THE BROWNIES IN HOSPITAL

PAMELA SYKES

The Brownies in hospital

Illustrated by Janina Ede

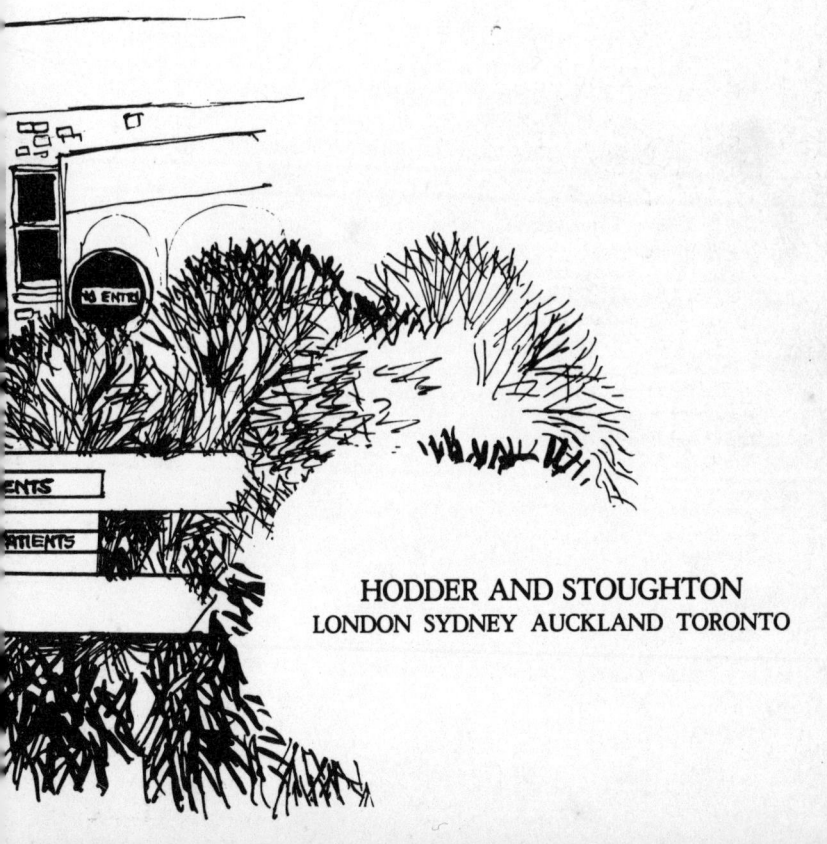

HODDER AND STOUGHTON
LONDON SYDNEY AUCKLAND TORONTO

For Juliet Jones

ISBN 0 340 17795 0

Text copyright © Pamela Sykes 1974
Illustrations copyright © Brockhampton Press Ltd 1974

First published 1974 by Brockhampton Press Ltd
(now Hodder and Stoughton Children's Books)
Third impression 1987

All rights reserved. No part of this publication may be
reproduced or transmitted in any form or by any means,
electronically or mechanically, including photocopying,
recording, or any information storage and retrieval system,
without either the prior permission in writing from the
publisher or a licence, permitting restricted copying, issued
by the Copyright Licensing Agency, 7 Ridgmount Street,
London WC1E 7AA.

Published by Hodder and Stoughton Children's Books,
a division of Hodder and Stoughton Ltd,
Mill Road, Dunton Green, Sevenoaks, Kent TN13 2YJ

Printed in Great Britain by T. J. Press (Padstow) Ltd,
Padstow, Cornwall

Contents

Chapter		
1	Preparations	7
2	Shopping	18
3	Accident	28
4	Left behind	40
5	Jane's idea	52
6	The unwelcome package	64
7	New ideas	76
8	Surprises	86
9	Home-coming	98
10	Looking forward	109

1 · Preparations

'Come on in,' invited Tracey, 'but wipe your feet first. Mum's a bit funny about things like that.'

Jane obediently slid her feet up and down the prickly mat outside the back door and followed Tracey into the kitchen.

'Good evening, Mrs Robinson,' she said politely to Tracey's mum who was putting a heavy-looking covered dish on the laid table.

'Hello, Jane,' she answered, her face pink and damp from cooking. 'Have a good meeting?'

'Marvellous,' said Jane, her own face glowing at the memory of the Brownie meeting she and Tracey had just attended. 'Miss Anderson was telling us —'

'— all about the Pack Holiday!' Tracey broke in. 'Just imagine! A week in the real country! She was making sure we'd got absolutely all the things we ought to have ready to take with us, and —'

The Brownies in hospital

'— and that they're named —' Jane put in.

'Yes, everything!' Tracey agreed. 'Even our knife and spoon and fork —'

'— and flannel and mug and toothbrush —'

Preparations

'And are they?' Mum removed another dish from the oven.

'Mine are,' said Jane, making room for the dish on the crowded table.

'Mine are *almost*,' said Tracey.

Mum put a string of loose hair behind her ear. 'Except for what?'

'Well, my pyjamas aren't, or my gumboots.'

'But you said you'd do those —'

'I know,' Tracey agreed hastily. 'And I will. It's just that I haven't had time yet. I had to see that everyone else in my Six had done theirs, so —'

'— so you didn't have time to see to your own?'

'Well, sort of,' said Tracey, and added, 'it *is* baked beans and bacon and sausages, isn't it? You said it would be.'

'And it is. Where's Johnnie?' Johnnie was Tracey's younger brother.

'Making a plasticine giraffe,' said Mr Robinson, coming in at that moment. 'Or a cow. I'm not sure which. Anyway's he's spreading a proper mess.'

'Not on the best table?' Mum said in an exasperated voice. 'You didn't *let* him?'

'I didn't stop him,' admitted Dad. 'Anything for a quiet life, that's what I say.'

The Brownies in hospital

'Because *you* don't have to polish the table after he's been modelling on it,' retorted Mum, bustling into the sitting-room to sort out Johnnie.

Tracey made a face at Jane, then laughed. 'Don't mind! Johnnie's always up to something, and Mum's always carrying on. She's quite used to it really. You sit there, and I'll be next to you. Dad, do you know it's only three days till the Pack Holiday?'

'Three days, is it really?' said Dad seating himself at the end of the table. 'All organized, are you?' He smiled at Jane. She nodded.

'Practically,' said Tracey.

'Practically?' Mr Robinson echoed. 'Except for what?'

'Oh, just some naming of things,' said Tracey airily. 'And I haven't got a rucksack yet.'

'But I told you you could buy one weeks ago!' her father protested.

'Yes. Well. I've been busy. And I haven't seen one I really like yet. And when you said I could look for one I was bang in the middle of taking my Athlete badge.'

'Not every minute of the day, you weren't.'

'But there's school!'

'There's always something, it seems to me. I thought your motto was "Be Prepared".'

Preparations

'Oh, Dad! That just shows how little you know about Brownies! That's the *Guide* one, not ours.'

'So what's yours?'

'"Lend a Hand",' said Tracey and Jane together.

Dad looked at Jane. 'Then you might lend a hand by helping to see this girl of mine buys a rucksack.'

'I'll try,' said Jane, smiling. Although she was shy of most people, she didn't mind Mr Robinson's teasing ways. She was used to them.

'I don't need *her* to tell *me* what to do!' exploded Tracey indignantly.

'No? Then how come she's got her rucksack and you haven't?'

Tracey was saved from answering this awkward question by the arrival of her mother holding Johnnie's wrist between two fingers, and leading him towards the sink.

'Just you get those hands clean at once! Tea's on the table. *And* we've got a visitor!'

'Only Jane,' said Johnnie comfortably. 'You don't mind if my hands are a bit liony, do you?'

Jane smiled but kept quiet. Mr Robinson said. 'Liony? I thought it was a giraffe?'

'Not enough plasticine for the neck,' explained Johnnie, turning on the cold tap.

The Brownies in hospital

'Why not?' said Tracey. 'You're only being nasty because you wish you could come with us.'

'Of course,' said Mum. 'Perfectly natural. More tea, anyone?' She refilled all the cups. 'Never mind, Johnnie. You shall go away with the Cubs as soon as you're old enough. Tracey, you'd better get those things marked this evening.'

'Can't,' said Tracey. 'I've got to draw a map.'

'When for?' asked her mother suspiciously.

'Tomorrow morning. First lesson after prayers. Isn't it, Jane?'

Jane nodded.

'You got to do one too?' Mr Robinson asked her.

'No. I've done mine.'

'When?'

'Um – yesterday. No, the day before. I forget.'

Mr Robinson looked at his daughter. 'So you've left your homework till the last minute again?'

'Brownie night, too. You are a nitwit,' said Mrs Robinson.

Tracey began to champ up her chocolate biscuit rather fast with pink cheeks.

'Tell you what,' said Jane to no one in particular. 'She can do her map and I'll name her things.'

'No you don't,' said Mum and Dad together.

Preparations

'She must do her own jobs for herself,' said Mum.

'Especially as she's a Sixer,' said Dad.

Tracey turned pinker. Johnnie ate happily with his mouth open and nobody noticed.

'But I am her Second,' said Jane. 'I'm supposed to help her.'

'Not with this sort of thing,' said Mum firmly.

Dad put some coins on the tablecloth by Tracey. 'See that you get that rucksack on Saturday.'

'Thanks, Dad,' said Tracey gratefully. 'Jane, will you come with me and help me look?'

'I thought you wanted me to come and pretend to test your skipping in the park?'

'I do. As well. We can easily do both, can't we, Mum?'

'If you're sensible about time and the traffic. You don't want to be in a hurry on a Saturday. The High Street gets jammed.'

'We'll start early,' Tracey promised.

'And me?' Johnnie asked, without much hope.

'You wouldn't like helping me skip *or* buy a rucksack,' said Tracey. 'You know you wouldn't. Dad, Miss Bennett at school said I'll be ready to take my Swimmer badge before the end of term, if I work hard.'

'Fancy,' said Dad.

The Brownies in hospital

Mrs Robinson turned to Jane. 'And what badges are you working for?'

Jane looked at her plate. 'Not difficult ones like Tracey. I've got my Needleworker and I'm working for Animal Lover, but I'm not very sportish, I'm afraid.'

'It doesn't matter what you're good at,' said Mrs Robinson, 'as long as it's something. Sometimes I wish Tracey would try for one of the less energetic kind of badges.'

'Like what?' asked Tracey suspiciously.

'Well – Book Lover or Writer, perhaps.'

'Mum you *know* I don't like reading! As for writing!'

'As for writing indeed,' her mother agreed. 'When I think of the song and dance we have over Christmas thank-you letters!'

'"Song and Dance!"' exclaimed Tracey, full of new ideas. 'There's a Dancer badge, but its awfully difficult unless you go to proper classes. I think I might be better at the Jester. You can dance in that.' Then she looked doubtful. 'You have to recite a poem too . . .'

Johnnie suddenly tipped his chair so far backwards that it almost fell over. His mother clutched at it. 'What are you *doing*?'

'Well!' said Johnnie in disgust. 'All this Brownie

Preparations

stuff! We haven't talked about anything else all tea time!'

'But it *is* terribly exciting!' Tracey pointed out. 'Especially if you've never stayed away from home before.'

'And there are only a few more days,' said Jane.

'A few more days!' said Tracey. 'However shall we get through them? I feel as if getting to that Pack Holiday is the only thing in the world I really want to do!'

2 · *Shopping*

'— Fifty-eight, fifty-nine, *sixty*!' cried Tracey triumphantly, and stopped skipping. It was a blue and gold hot day. The grass in the park was yellowed by sun, the paths dry as dust.

Tracey collapsed on the ground. She was scarlet in the face. 'You can have a go,' she suggested, holding out her skipping-rope towards Jane.

'You know I can't. I've tried and tried. It's just not my kind of *thing*.'

'It might be if you practised.'

But Jane sat on the ground too. 'You didn't say that when I asked you to take Needleworker with me!'

'Oh, *that*! I can't sew. Whatever stitch I try to make, they all come out the same, just loops and squiggles. And the thread gets grey and ties itself into knots on purpose.'

'There you are then. Sewing's not your thing and running-about badges aren't mine.' Jane lay back,

Shopping

closed her eyes, and opened them again. 'Have you noticed how if you squeeze your eyes shut you see lovely coloured patterns?'

They practised this for a while. Tracey grew tired of the game first. 'Most of my patterns are dark red. It's this sun. Shall we go shopping now?'

'What about your handstands?'

'Too hot.'

'Or shoulder stands?'

'Worse.'

'You're lazy.'

'*You* tell *me* I'm lazy!' cried Tracey. 'What about you?' She bounced to her feet and gave Jane a gentle kick. 'Come on, I've got to get that rucksack.'

Jane honestly admired Tracey a great deal. Partly because she was such an energetic and efficient Sixer, always organizing people. Partly because she was so good at things which Jane herself was not. She was proud to be Second in Tracey's Six and only too willing to help her in any way she might be asked. So now she climbed good-naturedly to her feet, quite prepared to hunt the dusty streets until the rucksack had been found.

There were several shops in the High Street which stocked the type of thing they were looking for, but Tracey was very fussy about the exact model.

The Brownies in hospital

'There we are!' Jane said hopefully the first time they saw a rucksack in a window.

'Too big,' said Tracey briefly, hardly pausing to inspect it. 'It's the kind of thing you see hikers wearing, all bent over because they're so heavy.'

'You wouldn't have to fill it so full that . . . ' Jane began, but Tracey had already plunged into another shop, one which sold camping equipment. There they were shown several different rucksacks, but Tracey had an objection to each.

'Too small. Much.'

'Not waterproof.'

'Too big again.'

The shop assistant began to look bored and Jane couldn't help sympathizing with him. Her own sandals were feeling far too full of hot feet. She longed to leave the stuffy shop and the glare of the streets, stopping perhaps to buy an ice-lolly on the way home. An ice-lolly! The more she thought of one, the drier her mouth became. One of those bright green lime ones. Or perhaps a blackcurrant, so sharp and tangy. On the other hand there was little to beat good old orange . . .

The assistant wearily produced another rucksack.

'No, thank you very much,' said Tracey.

Shopping

At last she was persuaded to try it on.

'Fits you perfectly,' said Jane, wondering if lime might not be the best after all.

'And anyhow, the straps are adjustable,' said the assistant.

'No, honestly —'

'And it's not too big,' said the assistant.

'Or too small,' said Jane.

'But the *colour*!' cried Tracey in tones of horror. 'Imagine what it would look like worn with Brownie-coloured brown and yellow?'

And Jane imagined. The rucksack was a bright blue. She could see what Tracey meant. She moved her weight from her left foot to her right and drew a slow breath. 'Perhaps you're right, but it will be just the job when you move up into the Guides, and meanwhile does it matter so much?'

'Yes, it does!' Tracey snapped. 'It might not to you, but it would to me. Miss Anderson expects me to set a good example and look just right. I'm a Sixer, remember?'

As if she ever forgot! And of course Tracey was right, as usual. Jane leant on her left foot again. It wouldn't much matter what her own equipment looked like, but everyone would expect Tracey's to look just right.

The Brownies in hospital

They said thank you to the assistant who was very polite about saying 'Not at all. It was a pleasure.'

'It can't really be a pleasure though,' Jane said, as they left the shop. 'Now he's got to put them all away again.'

'He won't mind,' said Tracey easily. 'After all, it's his job and he chose his job so I expect he likes getting things out and putting them away again. Mum's a bit like that with the airing cupboard and the kitchen shelves.'

Jane didn't agree with Tracey's views, but although she was rather cross and very hot, she was determined not to quarrel. Instead of arguing, therefore, she said encouragingly, 'If we get a move on we'll be able to get an ice-lolly at the corner shop.'

'What d'you mean, "Get a move on"?' said Tracey. 'We're going to get this rucksack, aren't we? Unless,' her voice, too, showed signs of exasperation, 'you think a rotten old ice-lolly is more important than my rucksack?'

Just for a moment, Jane did. She slid Tracey a sideways glance and realized at once that one more remark from either of them might result in a silly disagreement which would be a disastrous way for a Sixer and her Second to begin a holiday. To avoid saying anything at

Shopping

all, she began to walk faster. Tracey made no particular effort to keep up with her, and the bustling crowd on the pavement didn't help. Jane had nearly reached the pedestrian crossing that led to their way home when she thought she heard Tracey shout:

'Jane! Jane!'

'She only wants to say she's sorry she was such a fusspot and she'd really like an ice-lolly as much as I would', thought Jane without looking back. She can say that in a minute where it's less crowded. Although it was a crossing she practised her kerb drill. Bother, a blue lorry, going far too fast and paying no attention to the black and white stripes on the road! She'd have to begin all over again.

'Jane, come back!'

This time she was sure it was Tracey calling, but she wasn't going back now. She looked carefully up and down the road.

At last the traffic, obedient to the Highway Code, had slowed to an unwilling stop. Jane, in company with the little crowd around her, crossed safely to the other side of the High Street.

Once on the opposite pavement she stood back against a shop window to wait for Tracey. Another little knot of people was already gathering at the far side of

The Brownies in hospital

the crossing, and although she couldn't see her, Jane was sure Tracey would be in it.

Then she heard the cry again.

'Jane – look!'

What with the people passing and re-passing her and the noise of the passing traffic it was difficult to tell exactly where the voice came from. Then Jane saw Tracey, still on the far pavement, pointing with triumph into a shop window. Distantly Jane could make out a display of handbags, some smart, some casual, some ... yes, some were not bags at all, but rucksacks. And one, clearly the object of Tracey's thrilled interest, was not too big, not too small, and made of nice chestnut canvas, an excellent Brownie colour.

The traffic paused. The tidal surge of pedestrians hurried across the road. A car, and then another moved across the temporarily empty crossing.

Tracey suddenly saw Jane. No doubt of it. Jane saw, and always remembered, the way her face lighted with recognition.

She shouted something else which Jane didn't hear.

She waved an excited hand towards the shop window.

She started to run, bumping, jostling, looking neither left nor right.

Shopping

'Use the crossing!' cried Jane, even before she'd actually seen the danger.

But Tracey didn't hear her agitated voice or see her warning signal. As usual, when she was alight with an idea or a scheme there was no room in her mind for anything else. Quite regardless of approaching vehicles she ran on – and on —

'No!' yelled Jane. 'Wait!'

Afterwards she worried in case her violently waving arm should have looked like a beckoning signal. Or if Tracey had not even noticed it.

Certainly she didn't waver. Her long strong legs carried her in a leap off the pavement and into the road. Along which were thundering several cars, and a motor-cycle.

'Look out!' shrieked Jane.

Too late.

Tracey, conscientious Sixer as she was, had evidently forgotten all she had ever learned about the safe crossing of roads.

She never even glanced at the on-coming cars.

She began to sprint straight across the road.

There was a terrible screaming. Jane never knew if it came from the brakes of the traffic.

Or from those onlookers close to her.

Shopping

Or only from her own throat.

One second, Tracey, a bright figure in fawn shorts and a green shirt, seemed to be flying along under the very noses of the shiny cars. Then next, she was lying in the grey road, a little huddled heap.

She didn't even try to struggle to her feet.

She lay perfectly still.

3 · Accident

It seemed as if hours and hours passed, but it was probably only a few seconds before Jane was able to think at all.

At first she only felt sick, and as if her feet were growing solidly out of the pavement like a tree's roots.

Then everything she saw wavered, as if she were looking at a film taken by someone who had not held the cine-camera steadily enough.

Then the scene recovered from its vague, shimmery state into a proper picture again. Jane saw that the traffic had stopped. The driver – a man – of the black car nearest Tracey was climbing out very slowly. His face looked like tissue paper. People all round were staring and pointing.

Jane tried to think.

She tried to think calmly.

She tried to think like a Brownie.

Accident

Because she had studied the Brownie Guide Handbook often, little bits of knowledge began to float into her frighteningly empty mind.

'Simple First Aid. Cuts and grazes.'

But Tracey needed more than simple first aid, she was sure.

'A tip about Adhesive Dressings.' No good.

'Clothes on Fire.' Inappropriate.

There was a bit about crossing a road safely, but it was too late to think about that.

Then what . . . ?

Her knees felt shaky. She pulled at herself in exactly the sharp way you might pull up a knee-sock to remove the wrinkles.

Suddenly the wrinkles in her mind were straightened, and she was able to think again. She might not be a Sixer, but she was a Second. And no Brownie, let alone a Second, lost her head in an emergency. The driver of the black car was crouching over Tracey. Tracey lay still. Everyone was exclaiming. But no one seemed to be *doing* anything.

So she must. But what? Suddenly she knew what. Once she knew, her feet felt less like the roots of a tree and more like feet made for carrying a person from one place to another.

The Brownies in hospital

Fifty metres down the road was the Post Office. Outside it was a public telephone-box. As her now more sensible feet began to dash towards it, her hands – Brownie hands once more – felt in the zipped pocket of her jeans for the price of the local call. Yes, there it was, the tenpence she always carried just in case.

There was nobody in the telephone box so she was able to bang her way into its stuffy interior. Her hands shook as she laid the all-important coin on the little shelf by the receiver.

Then, as her eye was caught by a notice, she remembered something else. Emergency calls were free. No need for the tenpence, then. Forcing her eyes and her brain to work slowly together she read the instructions which told her exactly how to make the call.

Her fingers were so shaky that it was difficult to fit them into the holes to dial, but she managed it. It seemed to take a long time. A voice asked which service she wanted – fire, police or ambulance?

'Ambulance please. Quickly. Oh, and police too, because there's been an accident.'

She wanted to run back to Tracey then, but the voice went on asking her things in a calm even tone. Her name? Her address? Where exactly was she now?

'In a telephone box or how could I be ringing you?'

The Brownies in hospital

Jane was becoming frantic with impatience. Only then, after she had explained that it was the High Street Post Office Box and the accident was very close, did she realize that of course the voice had been right. If she hadn't told it where the accident was, how would it know where to send the police and ambulance to?

She burst out of the booth and pounded back down the pavement. Already there seemed to be hundreds of people round the place where Tracey had been knocked down. Jane pushed and shoved her way towards the front of the little crowd. If anyone pushed back crossly she said, 'Excuse me, but I know her', and she was let by.

Tracey lay just as she had before. Several people were stooping over her in a concerned way. They seemed to be arguing.

'Much better move her on to the kerb,' said the driver of the car.

'Oh no,' said Jane quickly. 'Much best *not*!'

'And who might you be?' asked the driver in an angry voice.

'Jane. Tracey's my friend. I saw it happen.'

'You did, did you?' said the driver. 'Then you can just tell the police that she ran straight under the wheels – straight under – didn't even look – a few metres

Accident

from a crossing too – straight under ...' He didn't seem to be able to stop. Another of the men present took his arm and said something in a firm low voice.

'All right for you, mate,' answered the driver, mopping his wet forehead. 'Doesn't affect you, does it?'

Tracey lay huddled almost as if she were asleep. But one leg looked a funny shape: there was a bend where no bend should be, and her face was a dreadful green-grey.

'Tracey?' said Jane. She stretched out a hand to touch her, but at the last moment withdrew it quickly. Somehow she couldn't. It was Tracey, but not Tracey. 'I think we ought to be keeping her warm,' she said suddenly.

'Warm?' echoed somebody. 'On a boiling day like this?'

'*She's* not hot,' said Jane stubbornly. 'Look at her.'

'Might be something in what the kid says,' said a woman. 'I saw a film about it on telly. Part of treatment for shock, or something.'

'That's it!' said Jane, remembering. They'd spent a whole Brownie meeting on first aid of all kinds. Miss Anderson had explained what 'shock' after an accident meant, and Jane could hear her voice now: 'Keep the patient warm.' She had also said. 'Comfort and soothe her. Don't move her. Fetch a grown-up quickly.' Well,

Accident

Jane had done what she could about that, but she couldn't comfort or soothe poor Tracey. If only she could! She stared at her poor pale face. A kind woman said, 'Don't take on dearie. They're never as bad as they look.'

A man had fetched an old coat from the back of his van. They spread it over Tracey. 'A bit oily, I'm afraid,' said the man apologetically, 'but better than nothing. Here, somebody ought to send for an ambulance.'

'I have,' said Jane.

'What?' said the woman. 'Already? There's a bright girl, then.'

Now that the first shock of the accident was over, everyone was beginning to behave more sensibly.

One man stood right in the middle of the busy High Street directing the traffic. Another was talking steadily to the driver, who was sitting half in and half out of his car with his head in his hands. 'He's shocked too,' thought Jane. And he's being comforted and soothed.

Several people were holding back the crowd. 'She must have air,' a voice kept saying. 'Give her air.'

'What about the kiss of life then?' asked another voice.

Jane remembered about the 'kiss of life', the name people gave mouth-to-mouth artificial respiration. Miss

The Brownies in hospital

Anderson had promised she would try to get them a model to practise on. Then she remembered it was only for if the patient had stopped breathing. Tracey was breathing all right. You could see her green shirt moving in and out. That was something to be thankful for.

But oh dear, *where* was the ambulance?

'Still think we ought to get her out of the road,' a new voice was arguing above Jane's head. 'Traffic's piling up and, anyway, we could make the kid more comfortable.'

'But don't you see – she doesn't know – so she doesn't care!' cried Jane. 'And I'm sure we shouldn't move her. Suppose she's got broken bones – we could make them worse. Or she may be hurt inside.'

'Here, how d'you know so much?' asked the man who had produced the coat. 'You a first-aider or a Guide or something?'

'Brownie,' said Jane. 'I'll be a Guide next year.'

'Come on, let's get her moved,' shouted the bossy man.

'Not on,' Jane's new friend shouted back. 'We've got a Brownie here. She says not to and she know's what's what.'

'Oh, I don't!' cried Jane, horrified that he should

Accident

think her an expert. But before anyone could say another word there came the sound Jane had been waiting for, the whoo! whoo! of an ambulance siren.

She stood up shakily, and saw the flashing blue light. Two uniformed men jumped out of the ambulance carrying a stretcher. Another car arrived. Police. Suddenly the frightening, lost feeling of no one being sure what to do was over. The real experts were in charge.

It was marvellous to see how carefully and gently Tracey was put on to the stretcher. Then it was lifted and slid into the back of the ambulance.

Somebody touched her arm and a policeman was beside her. 'Friend of yours?'

Jane nodded, still staring at the still form on the stretcher. (How would that man get his coat back?)

The ambulance doors were closed. Tracey going all by herself to a strange hospital. 'Please, I'd like to go with her.'

The policeman was kind but firm. Tracey was unconscious, and the right people to be with her when she came round were her father and mother. Could Jane give their name and address? She did so. The policeman leant into his car to give a radio message

The Brownies in hospital

from it. 'One of our kind police ladies will go straight round to tell them now,' he said.

Jane thought of Tracey's mum's face when she heard. She swallowed.

'You feeling all right?' the policeman asked.

Jane nodded, but doubtfully. Now that she had time to think about it, she realized she was feeling very wobbly.

'Just a few questions, then,' said the policeman, 'and then home's the place for you.'

She gave her own name and address and told in a few words what had happened. 'We'll call on you later for details,' the policeman said. 'Sure you're all right? Or would you like a lift home in one of our cars?'

'No! I mean, no *thank* you,' said Jane. She wanted to get away from all this as soon as possible. She edged through the thinning crowd. Her wobbly legs took her home all by themselves. She was quite surprised to find herself there.

Mum opened the door and took one look at her face. 'What's happened? What's wrong?' she asked sharply as she drew her indoors.

'Tracey. She was hit by a car. She's on her way to hospital. Mum, I'm going to be sick, quick . . .'

Afterwards, sitting down with a cup of tea, she was

Accident

able to describe everything more calmly, though by the end of her story she found tears dripping into her tea, and her teeth chatting.

'S-s-tupid!' she managed, 'Anyone'd have th-thought it was me.'

'It *was* you,' said her mother hugging her. 'You've had as much shock as any of them, but you've done your bit, so now I'm going to put a bottle in your bed and you can have a lie down. Once you're in, I'll just nip round to Tracey's mum and see if *I* can lend a hand!'

4 · Left behind

Later, Tracey was able to recall only blurred memories of what happened next.

Of the actual accident she knew nothing at all. Her last memory was of seeing the rucksack – *the* rucksack she'd seen in the shop window, and knowing at once it was the one she wanted. She'd turned excitedly to point it out to Jane, and then – blank.

The next thing of which she was aware was of a curious lurching sensation and occasional jolts. The jolts hurt her left leg. She opened her eyes and met those of a darkly-uniformed man with red hair, sitting beside her.

He grinned at her in a friendly way. 'Hello, love.'

She frowned. 'Hello.' Her voice came out only as a whisper.

There came another jolt. Tracey winced.

'Where's it hurt?' her companion asked.

'My leg.'

Left behind

'Never mind – we'll be at the hospital in a minute.'

That was when she realized they must be going along. 'How?'

'You're in an ambulance.'

An *ambulance*!

She was actually inside an ambulance. How exciting! She meant to ask, 'Is its siren going? And its light?' and 'How did I get here?' but suddenly it was all too much trouble. The red-headed man's face wavered and faded. Her heavy-lidded eyes dropped . . .

Time passed.

She was aware of the smell before she opened her eyes again. A strong smell, rather like Mum's first-aid cupboard; a little like the swimming pool.

'Ooph,' she murmured faintly, wrinkling her nose.

'Hello, Tracey,' said a voice.

A man in a white coat was standing beside the hard bed on which she lay. He had a square face that hid a half-smile, and the kindest eyes she'd ever seen. He made a movement and she winced again, afraid he was going to touch her leg.

'Where does it hurt?' he asked.

'My leg. This one.'

'Can you tell me where?'

She thought hard. 'No. All over.'

The Brownies in hospital

'Right up here?'

'No, lower down – don't! Please don't.'

'Don't worry, I don't want to hurt you. How about that shoulder?'

She was surprised. 'What shoulder?'

'You had a nasty bang on that right one.'

She tried to squint at it, but without success.

'How's the head?'

'I'm not sure.'

'What's your name?'

'Tracey. You said it just now.'

'So I did. Can you remember your address?'

'Of course. Number five, Shetland Terrace.'

'Well done.'

'But of course I know where I live. Can you stop my leg hurting?'

'Certainly. In a minute. I'll just take a look at that shoulder first. Nurse, scissors please.'

Tracey turned her head cautiously. For the first time she realized there was a grey-haired nurse standing quietly beside her. Also that the three of them were in a small white-curtained cubicle.

'Where is this?'

'The General Hospital. Keep quite still a moment, Tracey.'

Left behind

Tracey kept quite still as asked in spite of the flash of scissors. But a moment later she said indignantly. 'Here, you can't cut my shirt! It was new last week!'

'Sorry,' said the doctor. 'I've got to have a look at this shoulder of yours.'

'It's my leg that's worst. Nearly ten pounds that cost, and I've to look after it, Mum said.'

But the doctor was calmly snip-snipping away at the sleeve of the shirt, taking no notice of her protests. 'You've had a bang here,' he explained, 'and a nasty graze.' He peeled the tattered edges of the shirt away from the hurt place. 'Mmm, you'll have a beautiful bruise in a day or two.'

But Tracey was only worrying about a ruined shirt. 'It was a size too big on purpose, so that it would *last* – I wish my Mum was here.' As soon as she had said that, she forgot about the shirt and could only think of how very much she wished Mum were there.

The nurse was called away for a few minutes, then returned to murmur something to the doctor.

'Back in a moment, Tracey,' said the doctor and left the cubicle. While he was gone the nurse talked quickly asking Tracey how much she could remember of the accident and if she had any aches or pains anywhere else she hadn't mentioned.

43

The Brownies in hospital

Tracey answered she could remember nothing, her leg hurt most though her shoulder was beginning to, 'and my head feels most queer. As if half my face wasn't there. And things come and go a bit. Sometimes you're close, and sometimes just a voice far away.'

'That will come right in no time,' said the nurse, 'it's only because you had a jolly good bump on that head of yours. And —'

The doctor returned. He was smiling. 'Well, Tracey, your wish has come true! Your Mum *is* here! Like to see her?'

'Yes, *please* – if you don't mind.'

'I don't mind at all about *your* Mother.'

'But you do about some?'

'The not-so-sensible ones.'

Tracey was interested. 'What sort of not-so-sensible?'

'You'd be surprised. Some talk in loud voices and disturb everyone else. They try to tell us what to do and what not to do, and argue with the hospital rules or try to take the patient home when he's not ready to go, or even say they won't allow us to do the best things to make them better —'

'But you're the doctors!' Tracey broke in, shocked. 'You're supposed to know —'

'Exactly. But there are just a few who aren't sensible

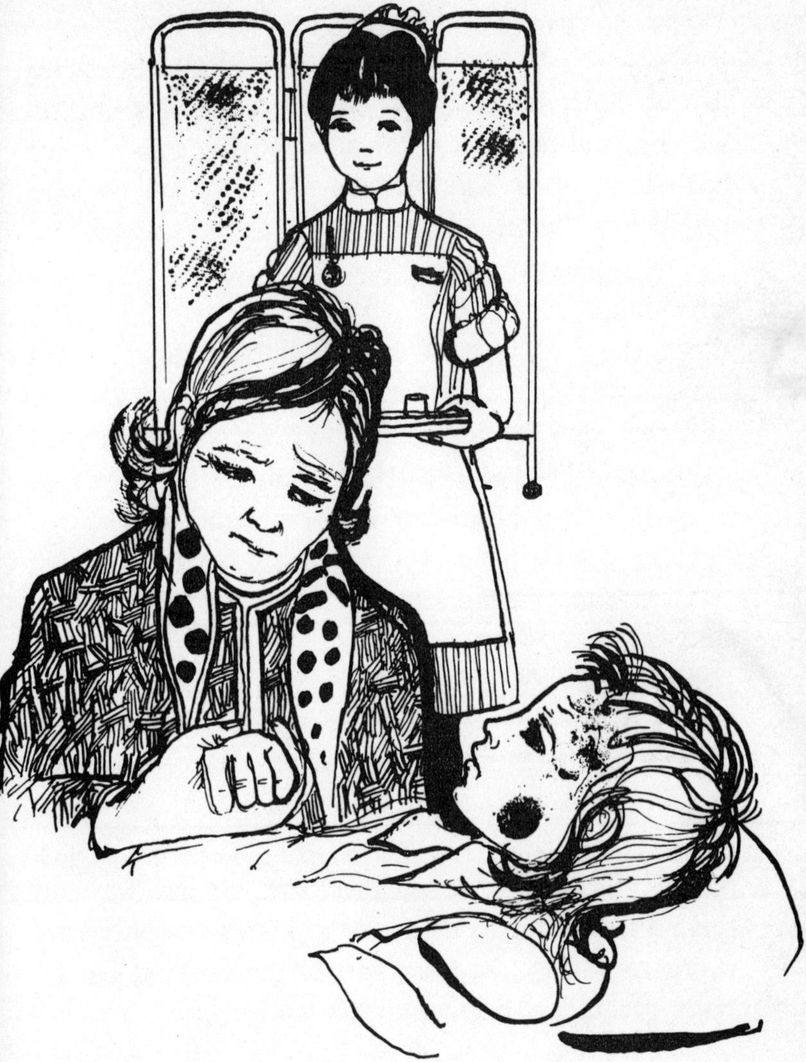

The Brownies in hospital

enough to realize that. Now your Mum's a model parent. She's been waiting quietly to know if she can see you, and now that I've explained you're not in too bad shape, she's only anxious for us to get on with making you better, and will do just as she's asked. She was very pleased to hear that you're being brave and sensible too.'

Somehow, though, it was difficult to go on being brave and sensible when she saw Mum, wearing her best coat, and looking so anxious. Tracey's eyes filled with tears. Then she saw that Mum's had too which made it worse. Mum just took her hand and held it tight for a little while without saying anything.

Then Tracey said, 'Mum, the doctor cut my new shirt.'

Mum's mouth gave a funny twist and she said *that* wasn't the end of the world, and after that there was hardly any time to talk because the doctor – whose name turned out to be Martin – said he'd like some X-ray photographs of Tracey straight away. Tracey opened her eyes wide at that, but Dr Martin said there was nothing to it, and what about not bothering Mum to walk to another part of the hospital but let nurse give her a nice cup of hot tea instead?

Tracey knew how much she would like the tea, so she

Left behind

nodded. The coming and going feeling was happening more now, so being wheeled away on a trolley and going in a lift on it, and keeping still while a machine photographed her seemed hardly important.

She heard Dr Martin tell her later. 'You're a lucky young woman. Things might have been a lot worse. Now we're going to make that leg much more comfortable, and we'll send you off to sleep while we do it. When you wake up you'll be in a warm bed.' Something cold was rubbed gently into Tracey's good arm. 'You'll just feel a tiny prick,' said the doctor. She did, but it *was* very tiny. 'Now, can you count up to ten?'

'One, two, three, four, five ... seven, eight ...' muttered Tracey, but got no further.

It seemed like the very next second when she opened her eyes and just as Dr Martin had promised, she was in bed. She felt the clothes warmly round her and stared at the ceiling, and shut her eyes and went back to sleep.

When she next awoke she felt more herself. She found a different nurse sitting on one side of her and Mum the other, smiling at her.

'Hello, Mum.'

'Hello, darling.' There was something a bit wrong with Mum's voice, but she went on smiling. 'Feeling better?'

The Brownies in hospital

Tracey thought about this for a little. 'Yes,' she said at last. 'I think so.' She tried to turn over to face Mum and found she couldn't. Her bad leg felt heavy as lead and her shoulder was as stiff as if it belonged to a wooden doll, not her at all. She put her free hand to her head and felt bandages instead of hair. She tried to think clearly and found she couldn't.

'Mum, what's wrong with me?'

'You were knocked over by a car. You might have been ...' Mum's voice faltered '... hurt much more badly. As it is, you've only broken a leg.'

'*Only!*' A broken leg sounded bad enough.

'And it will soon mend, Dr Martin said. And don't worry about your shoulder or your head. Nothing broken there. Only bad bumps. They'll be better in no time.' She made it sound as if Tracey was very lucky to have hurt her leg and her shoulder and her head. 'Dad'll be here in a minute,' Mum added.

'Dad? But – what's the time?'

'Nearly six.'

Nearly six! And she'd been shopping in the *morning*! Another thought came to her. 'But what about his tea? And Johnnie's?'

'Jane's mum's looking after them. She's been ever so kind.'

Left behind

'Another worry came back to Tracey. 'What'll Dad say about my new shirt?'

'Nothing. He's just glad to know you're all right. That's all that matters.'

'How does he know?'

'The Police rang him at work.'

'The Police! At *work*?'

'Of course.'

No of course about it. People weren't really allowed to ring Dad at the Bus Depot.

'But by that time, we knew you'd soon be right as rain,' Mum said. 'So there was no need for him to come at once.'

'How did you get here so quickly?'

'Police again,' said Mum, almost proudly. 'A very nice police lady came round and they brought me in a car.'

Tracey was impressed. 'I didn't know police were so kind.'

'Nor did I,' said Mum. 'Marvellous they were. Nothing too much trouble —' She broke off suddenly. 'Here's Dad!'

And there was Dad, looking a bit awkward beside the bed.

'Hello, Tracey,' he said.

The Brownies in hospital

'Hello, Dad.'

Mum said. 'She's doing fine, they say. Out of here in no time.'

'What's "no time"?' Tracey asked quickly.

Mum and Dad looked at each other quickly. Mum said, 'Not more than two weeks, anyway. Perhaps less.'

'Two weeks!' cried Tracey. 'But what about the Pack Holiday? That's in two *days*.'

'Yes, well . . .' said Dad. And stopped.

'You couldn't go on holiday with a broken leg, now could you?' Mum asked in a reasonable voice.

'But – but —' She couldn't miss it, she *couldn't*! Tracey wanted to sit up and explain, protest, scream, demand . . . Weighed down by plaster and bandage she could do none of these things. 'I must go! Oh, I *must*! Mum, you've got to explain.'

Dad cleared his throat.

'Darling,' said Mum. 'There's nothing to explain. You must stay here till you are well enough to come out, and by that time the Brownies will be back. I'm awfully sorry. We all are. But there's nothing to be done about it.'

No Pack Holiday! The thing they'd all been looking forward to for weeks and weeks. And nobody cared! Tracey turned her head away from her parents. Tears

Left behind

oozed out of her eyes. At first she cried quietly. Then sobbed more loudly. A nurse appeared. She, Mum and Dad talked reasonably to Tracey in quiet voices.

Tracey wouldn't listen. Not to a single word.

5 · Jane's idea

Life during the Pack Holiday was very busy.

'Who'd have thought that just cooking meals and eating them and washing up and going to bed and getting up could take so much time?' wailed Rosemary, a member of Tracey's Six.

Miss Anderson laughed. 'Now you know why your mothers never have a minute to spare!'

'But there are only five in our family.'

Jane's idea

'Five to care for, but only five to help. And perhaps they don't all help?'

'Well, Dad doesn't much. He's hardly ever in. And our Thomas is only four —'

'But they both need looking after, don't they? So you see —'

'Are you going to tell us again how important it is to lend a hand at home?' asked Rosemary suspiciously.

There was a general laugh from the group listening.

'No I'm not,' said Miss Anderson, 'because you've just discovered it for yourself.'

While they were talking, the Brownies were working. Today it was their Six's turn to prepare meals. Lunch was going to be a picnic, so that was easy: rolls, tomatoes and cheese and chocolate biscuits and huge red apples.

'But when everybody gets back after a day on the hills, they'll be starving!' Miss Anderson warned, so now potatoes and carrots were being scraped for the starving Brownies and later they'd be eaten with the meat, gravy and onion bubbling in big pans in the kitchen.

'It smells so good I feel as if I could eat it all myself – now this minute!' Rosemary exclaimed presently.

'You piglet!' came another voice. 'You've only just had breakfast!'

'That was *hours* ago!'

The Brownies in hospital

Miss Anderson looked at her watch. 'It was exactly fifty-six minutes ago.'

'Is that all?' said Rosemary in genuine amazement, and produced another laugh.

Jane concentrated on the carrot she was preparing. The holiday was fun. With seventeen Brownies determined to enjoy themselves it could hardly be anything else. They slept on camp-beds in long rows down the gleaming village hall. They ate meals they had cooked themselves in the little kitchen. Most of the time they were out of doors, exploring, picnicking, playing various games. Everything was aimed at giving them a good time.

But Tracey wasn't there.

All the time they had been planning today's meals, and getting them ready, Jane had been wondering what poor Tracey was being given to eat in hospital.

Ever since they had started the great holiday adventure, her thoughts had followed the same patterns. *How* Tracey would have enjoyed the train journey, the coach-trip from the village station, the bustling of settling in!

The first night little Sharon, the youngest of the Pack, had cried after they were all in bed and said she wanted to go home. It had been Jane who had heard her, and tried to comfort her and finally had to fetch Miss

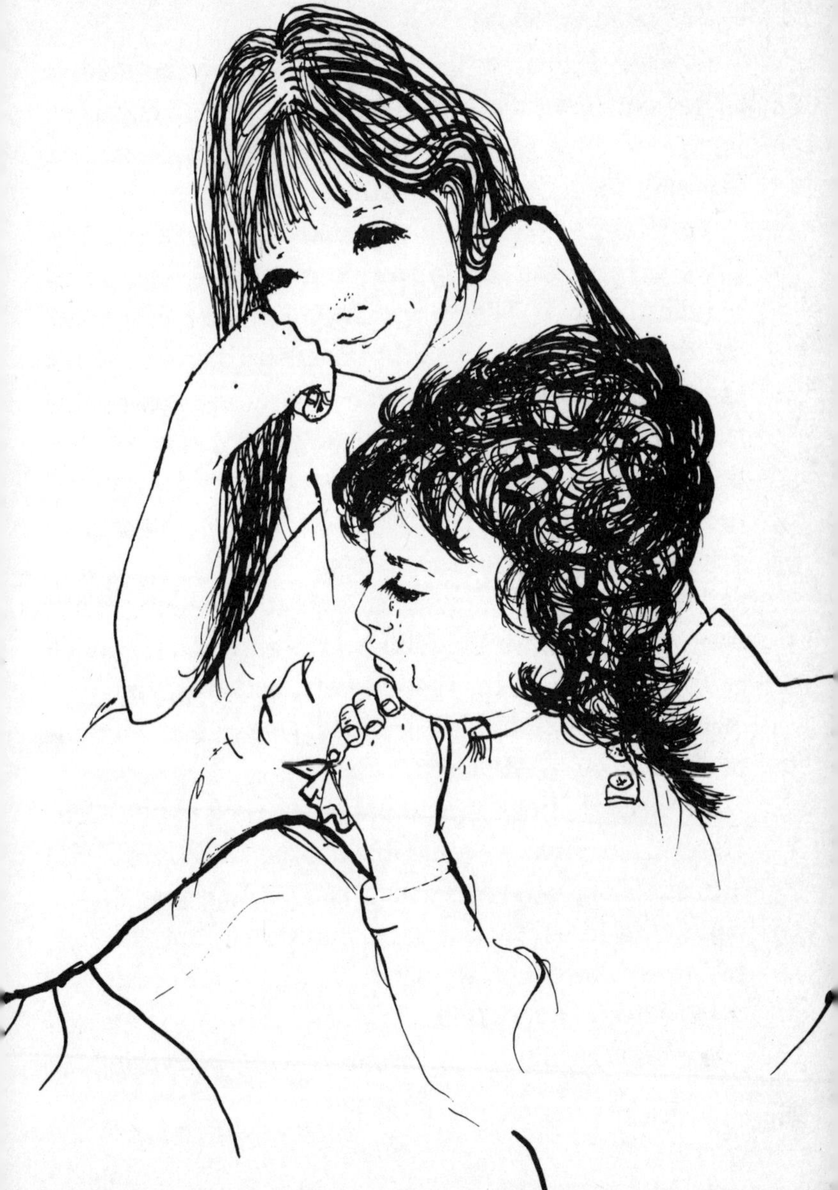

The Brownies in hospital

Anderson. Probably Tracey would have been able to calm poor Sharon all by herself. As Tracey had been unable to come Jane had to try to take her place. She was sure she was doing it badly.

Yesterday they had explored the village. The Brownies had had a competition to see who could find out most about it. Where was the post office? Where did the doctor live? Who could remember the name of the grocer's shop? Where did each road at the cross-roads lead to? When the marks were added up, it was found their Six was second. Miss Anderson said they had done very well. But Jane was sure that if Tracey had been there, they would have won.

Today's picnic should be tremendous fun. They were going to climb a big hill nearby and eat their lunch at the very top of it. Tracey, with her long, fast legs, would have loved it. Now she was lying in bed with one of them broken. Missing all the fun.

At the end of the week there were going to be sports. Here again Tracey would have been invaluable. Not just at telling everyone which competition they would enter, and in which race they would run, but she herself would have won so many events.

Oh, it did seem unfair.

And not having her here was spoiling everything.

Jane's idea

Someone had made another joke. People were laughing all round here. Jane remembered she had a job to do. Her hands, which had idled as she thought, became busy again with her carrot. As she scraped at its ridged outside she felt Miss Anderson looking at her. She scraped harder. It was bad enough not being as good a leader as Tracey would have been, without her Brownie Guider suspecting her of being lazy as well. She reached hastily for another carrot out of the basket.

Presently the three Sixes started from three different points at the foot of the hill. Then they had a race for the top. It was hot work scrambling up the steep slope, searching for the narrow worn tracks the sheep had made, to help them, grabbing at the tough grass. Jane was nearly there when she noticed Sharon was lagging far behind. Which should she do, Jane wondered? Dash for the summit and perhaps win the race for her Six? Or go back and help Sharon over the rough patches? It was a hard choice to make. What would Tracey have done? She only had to think for a second about *that*! She'd have dashed on and claimed victory.

But Jane could see Sharon's round face, scarlet and tearful far behind everyone else. It would be mean to leave her struggling alone. Regretfully, Jane slid back down the hill.

The Brownies in hospital

'Come on!' she called encouragingly as she stretched out her hand.

Sharon grappled it gratefully. There were still tears on her face. Jane was glad she'd gone back to help her.

But another Six reached the top first.

If Tracey had been here, that wouldn't have happened.

Miss Anderson had been quite right about everyone being hungry after a whole day in the open air. Well, almost right. For Jane found she didn't really want her first helping of the delicious stew. And certainly not a second.

Just before bedtime a nearly-round moon moved slowly over the hills. Everybody went outside the hall to breathe the sweet night air and to watch it.

'There's the Plough,' somebody said, pointing to the stars.

'Where?'

'Over there. It looks like a saucepan. And over the church —'

'Jane,' said Miss Anderson quietly.

Jane jumped. She hadn't realized the Brownie Guider was standing beside her. She hoped there weren't going to be questions about stars because she hadn't been attending to the talk going on round her.

Jane's idea

But Miss Anderson said, 'Worrying about Tracey isn't going to help her one bit, you know.'

'Oh!' said Jane. How did Miss Anderson know what her thoughts had been? 'It's difficult not to, though...'

'Of course it is. We all miss her, and wish she could be here. But as that's not possible it would be stupid to let her absence spoil things for the rest of us. She's in the best possible place being looked after, remember.'

'But she was so longing to come.'

'I know. And it's very disappointing for her. But disappointments happen to everyone sometimes. Meanwhile you must enjoy every minute of this holiday. It's the last one you'll have as a Brownie, remember. Don't waste a minute of it regretting what can't be helped.'

'The trouble is —' Jane began, and then stopped.

'Yes?'

'Well —' Jane found it rather difficult to go on. 'The thing is – you see —' she stopped again.

Miss Anderson said nothing.

Jane pressed on. 'If she'd been here, we – I mean our Six – would have done much better.'

'In what way?'

'At the competitions and games. Tracey is – was – so good at that sort of thing. And getting everybody to

The Brownies in hospital

join in properly. I'm sure she'd have got to the top of the hill first today for instance.'

'So might you, if you hadn't gone back to help Sharon,' said Miss Anderson.

Goodness! she seemed to know everything!

'But Tracey will ask how many things we won, and so far its nothing and she'll think —'

'— you've let her down? If she does, she'll be quite wrong,' said Miss Anderson. 'You've done splendidly, Jane. You've sorted everyone out and helped the little ones and worked hard and generally done everything a Sixer should. Except perhaps look cheerful. Look, if you want to do something practical so that Tracey doesn't feel so left out, why don't you write her a letter? Tell her all about everything we're doing?'

'It would be a terrifically long letter,' said Jane. 'I know, perhaps we could each write. Everybody about something different.'

'That's a very good idea.'

'And Rosemary could draw the things that have happened. She's awfully good.'

'Better still,' said Miss Anderson.

Jane began to feel more cheerful. If Tracey got lots of letters she'd know they hadn't forgotten her. 'If we started tomorrow, we could do it for several days, like a

Jane's idea

diary. And reading it all would give her something to do in bed.' The more she thought of the scheme, the happier she felt. 'Could you please explain the plan to everyone?' she asked Miss Anderson.

'Why not you? It was your idea.'

'You thought of the letter.'

'But you thought of everything else. I'm sure the rest of the Pack will be only too glad to join in.'

'But – but—' Jane couldn't see herself organizing something like this. Tracey wouldn't have hesitated. Jane could imagine her getting everyone to listen, describing enthusiastically what she wanted done, reminding and encouraging and nagging ... But she, Jane, wasn't that kind of person.

'No "Buts" about it!' Miss Anderson was saying with brisk cheerfulness. It's time to go in now. When everybody's ready for bed you can get them together.'

And that's what happened. To her own surprise Jane found her quiet voice just as effective as Tracey's louder one. The Pack listened carefully while she explained about the letters, declared it a good idea and promised to start the very next day. Someone suggested including some pressed flowers. Someone else said the photos she had taken of the first day would soon be developed and they could send one of those. Other

The Brownies in hospital

people besides Rosemary wanted to draw. It was exciting, Jane found, to discover people were so ready to join in.

Next day the letters were started. Some were rather short. Several were untidy, for most got written balanced on people's knees at odd moments. The various bits of news were divided up so that Tracey should hear of everything, but nothing twice. They visited the old village church that day and a postcard of it was included. Ann fell into a stream the following morning so somebody described that, and Rosemary drew a big coloured picture of it happening. Miss Anderson included a note of her own. By the time everything was collected together it made quite a big bundle. Miss Anderson bought a special big envelope to hold it all, and then posted it off to Tracey by first-class post so that she'd get it as soon as possible.

After that Jane felt much better. She stopped thinking of Tracey all the time. She joined in with whatever was happening with all her mind. She even stopped worrying about how much better Tracey would have managed everybody. When their Six came last in the sports, she didn't mind. After all, the afternoon had been tremendous fun even if they hadn't won.

The days rushed by, each faster, it seemed, than the

Jane's idea

one before. She could hardly believe it when it was time to go home. It was sad saying good-bye to all their village friends, to see the country change gradually into town as the coach took them all away from the green hills.

But once on their way, the Brownies began to look forward to getting home. They had so much to tell their families they could hardly wait to begin.

And on the very next day, Jane promised herself, she would go and visit Tracey in hospital.

6 · *The unwelcome package*

'Here's a package for you, Tracey!' said Nurse Davis cheerfully, as she laid something on Tracey's neat white bed and passed on to distribute other letters and parcels to people eagerly waiting for them.

Tracey only humped herself more deeply under the bedclothes. She didn't want a package. She didn't want anything. Just to be left alone. She screwed her eyes up to shut out the sight of the other beds and people in them. She pulled the sheets round her ears so that she couldn't hear the sounds of other children opening their post.

Some of those in the ward were too young to be sent letters. Sometimes they were sent presents instead. Or big drawings to make them laugh. If there was writing that was difficult to make out, the nurses would read the letters to the younger ones. Over and over again.

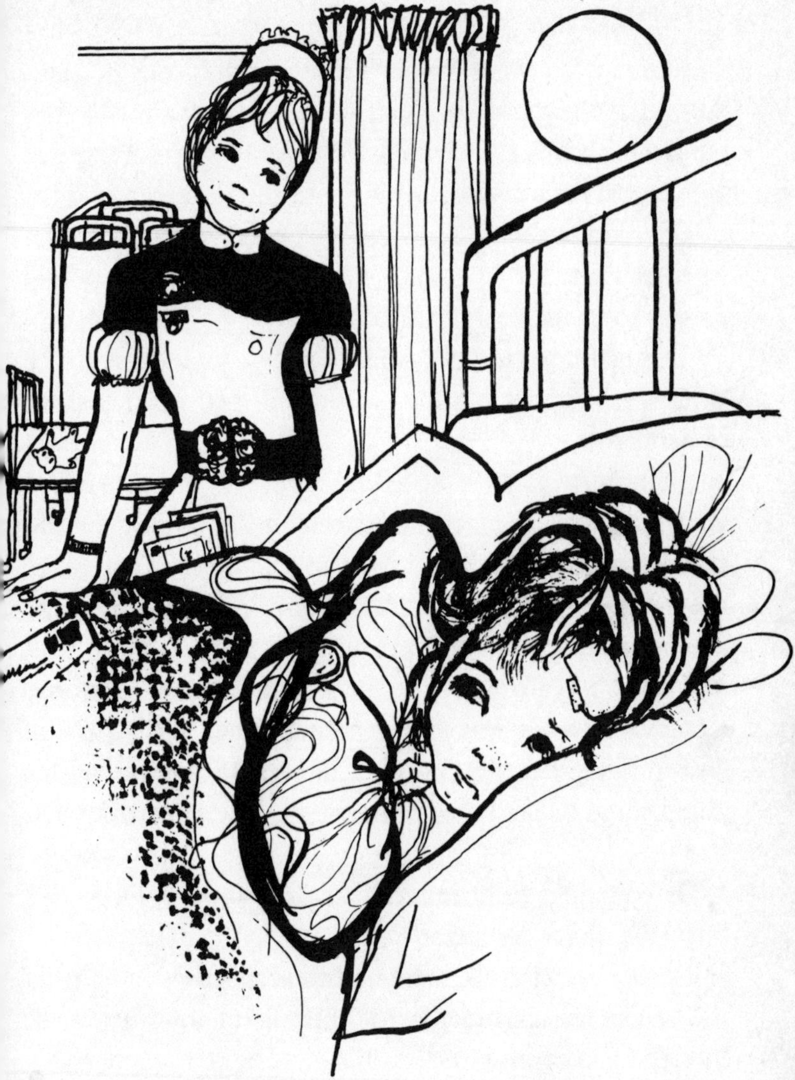

The Brownies in hospital

The nurses were kind. Tracey had to admit that. Although they had so much to do, looking after twenty children, they seemed never too busy to stop for a quick word or to have a joke, or play with the littlest ones.

The doctors were kind too. Especially Tracey's own 'special' one: Dr Martin. He came to see her every day to see how she was getting on.

'Doing fine,' he said, one morning, and he said she could have sticky plaster on her bumped head instead of bandages.

'Just look at this splendid bruise!' he exclaimed another morning when he examined her shoulders. He asked a nurse to fetch a mirror so that Tracey could see the bruise herself. It certainly was impressive: very large and blue and green and purple in patches.

'Looks like a storm at sea!' said Dr Martin, grinning. Tracey knew he was trying to make her smile, so she didn't. She had nothing to smile about, so she wasn't going to be tricked into pretending to be cheerful when she wasn't.

Dr Martin gently moved her arm about. 'Does this hurt? Or that? Or that?'

Tracey scowled, but she had to admit that in spite of the bruise her shoulder hardly hurt at all now. 'It's stiff, though,' she complained.

The unwelcome package

'That's because you haven't been using it,' said Dr Martin. 'As soon as you get up and about, it'll be itself again.'

'Up?' said Tracey. 'About? – How can I?' She glared at her leg. She knew now that its heaviness was caused by a thick white plaster cast which reached from above her knee almost to her toes.

'Easy as wink,' said the Doctor. Tracey, in her present mood, found him rather maddening. Nothing seemed to stop him being cheerful. Of course, it wasn't he who was in bed with a broken leg. He'd feel different if it was. 'Nothing to it, he went on, it's only a greenstick fracture after all.'

'Greenstick?' Tracey repeated. Any conversation that concerned herself was interesting, though she didn't want to hear about anyone or anything else.

'Don't you know what that means? You can probably guess, if you think.'

'No I can't,' said Tracey quickly, not even trying.

'Well, I'll explain. If an older person breaks a bone it's apt to go snap! like an old dry twig. Know what I mean?'

Tracey nodded.

'But have you ever tried to break a young green twig off a tree? It's difficult, isn't it? It'll bend, and give a

67

The Brownies in hospital

little, but it's hard to break off. Well, that's just how your bones are while you're still young. Difficult to break completely, just like a green stick. So they don't snap right through, and they very quickly mend.'

'Oh,' said Tracey, not sure whether to be pleased or sorry at this news. If she was going to have a broken leg at all, she wanted it to be properly broken. 'I still don't see how I can get *up*, though.'

'Not only up, but about,' said the doctor. 'We'll have you on crutches soon. It's only been your shoulder that's held you up. Now that's so much better, you'll be getting round the place in no time, making yourself useful.'

'Useful!' repeated Tracey, indignantly. 'I'm not going to be useful. I'm ill!'

The doctor actually laughed out loud in a most unfeeling way. 'You're not *ill*!' He went to visit the patient in the next bed.

That had been yesterday. She had been extremely annoyed. She'd show them she was ill, she decided. For the first few days in hospital she hadn't wanted to eat anything, and nobody had made her. Drinks were enough. Then soups and jelly and ice-cream had begun to appear. They were rather good, and Tracey secretly looked forward to meal-times. But if they were going to

The unwelcome package

make out that there was nothing wrong with her, she'd show them! And she was sure she wasn't well enough for crutches yet. As for making herself useful! She actually snorted with crossness as she burrowed even more deeply into her bed.

'What?' said Nurse Davis. 'Haven't you opened that packet yet?'

Tracey said nothing. It was a stupid question to ask. Anyone could see the package hadn't been touched since it had been put on her bed.

Nurse Davis sat down beside her. 'It looks interesting.'

'Leave it alone!' said Tracey sharply, though her voice was half muffled by bedclothes. 'It's mine.'

'Then I should open it, if I were you,' said the nurse pleasantly. She got up and went away.

Tracey frowned angrily to herself. You'd have thought that as she was lying ill in bed they could have at least opened that bulgy envelope for her. But no, though she waited for half the morning, nobody bothered. Tracey tried not to look at it but her eyes kept coming back to it. By turning her head and squinting, she could see the postmark: 'Westhill.'

Westhill! That was where the Brownies were!

She wanted to open the bundle. She didn't want to. She couldn't make up her mind. She nudged at it with

The Brownies in hospital

her good knee, hoping it might fall on to the floor. (Then somebody would have to pick it up for her.) But it didn't.

Nurse Davis came round with lunch trays. She helped to prop Tracey up against her pillows, and lifted the lid from her plate. Chicken and potatoes and cauliflower. It did smell good. But Tracey pushed it away, and in spite of a tummy that gurgled with hunger, she didn't take a bite.

It was even more difficult to resist treacle sponge, but she managed. When Nurse Davis came to take away the tray she said nothing about no dinner having been eaten. Or about the unopened package.

Tracey lay on her back and sulked all through rest time.

After tea, when Mum and Dad came to see her she had still not opened the package. She put it on the bed where they couldn't fail to see it.

Mum pounced on it at once. 'What's this? A lovely fat letter and you haven't opened it?'

'I don't want to,' Tracey muttered. 'It's from the Brownies.'

'But surely you want to hear what they're doing?' said Dad, surprised.

'Not a bit,' said Tracey. 'If I'm left out of everything,

The unwelcome package

why should I want to hear what *they're* doing? It only makes it worse.'

'That's a silly way of looking at it,' said Dad, ignoring Mum frowning at him. 'If they're kind enough to write to you – Here, give it to me, I'll open it if you won't!'

'You can't. It's mine!' said Tracey.

Dad began to slit open the package with his pen-knife just the same.

'Never mind,' Mum said quickly. 'Tell us, what did you have for dinner today?'

Just the question Tracey had hoped for. 'Nothing!' she said.

'Nothing!' Mum was scandalized. 'They should give you *something*, surely!'

'Oh, they did,' Tracey said. 'But I didn't feel well enough to eat it.'

Mum tch-tched but Dad only let a great pile of letters slide out of the envelope on to the coverlet. 'Look at this lot, then!'

Tracey looked and looked away quickly. She had time to glimpse different handwritings, some photos, some drawings ... She longed to examine them but was too proud.

'What about tea?' Mum wanted to know.

The Brownies in hospital

'Oh, the usual,' said Tracey in a bored voice. 'Bread and butter and jam, and a cake-thing ... I didn't try that either.'

Mum stood up. 'I'm going to speak to Sister.'

'Oh, don't!' cried Tracey. Sister was the head nurse in the ward and everyone was a little in awe of her. But Mum was already stumping off determinedly to inquire about meals. Tracey lay back uneasily.

'If you can't be bothered to read these, I'll read them to you,' said Dad. He unfolded a letter in a big sprawling writing. 'Dear Tracey' he read aloud. 'Hope you are well ...'

'Stupid,' said Tracey, 'of course I'm not, or I'd be there.'

'I had a bad wasp-sting,' Dad read on as if she hadn't interrupted. 'Miss Anderson put some stuff on it and it got better but now it – it – goodness, this spelling! – *now it itches!*'

'Who's it from?' Tracey couldn't resist asking.

Dad turned the page over. 'Somebody called Sharon,'

'Oh, *her!*' said Tracey in a scornful voice. But she thought: 'Poor little Sharon.'

'We had scrambled egg for breakfast,' Dad read from another letter, 'but Rosemary let it burn a bit ...' There

The unwelcome package

was a picture of the scrambled egg, apparently burning as fiercely as a bonfire on Guy Fawkes night. Tracey saw it out of the side of her eye.

Presently Mum finished her talk with Sister, and came back to the bed. 'You're doing very well, darling,' she told Tracey cheerfully.

'I'm not,' said Tracey at once. 'I can't eat. I'm not well enough.'

'Of course you are!' Mummy actually laughed in what Tracey thought a most unfeeling way. 'There's nothing much wrong with you now except for your leg and that won't take long.'

'But don't you – aren't they worrying that I can't eat?' Tracey asked.

'Not in the least,' said Mum cheerfully. 'Nobody is. Now I think it's time Dad and I went home.'

'Oh, must you?' Tracey's voice was almost a whine. 'You haven't been long.'

'But Johnnie's round with Jane's mum while we're here so we mustn't be too long. Besides, I'm not sure that you're in the mood for visitors.'

Tracey wasn't sure either. She didn't want her parents to go. On the other hand if they were going to spend the time telling her there was nothing much wrong with her —

The Brownies in hospital

'And you've got all these letters to read,' Dad reminded her.

'I don't want to,' said Tracey, and deliberately twitched the bedclothes so that the letters fell on to the floor.

Dad bent to pick them up.

'I should leave them there,' said Mum, 'if Tracey doesn't want to read them anyway.'

'Can't litter the place up,' Dad said cheerfully, as he straightened with his hands full of paper. He lowered his voice to ask Tracey 'What's wrong with that poor little chap on the other side of you, the one lying flat on his back?'

'I don't know.'

'And there's a girl over there with *both* legs in plaster,' Mum added quietly. 'What happened to her?'

'How can I tell?'

'It'll be nice when you're able to get about and talk to everyone,' said Mum, 'and find out!'

What a thing to say, thought Tracey, after they'd left, when it was she who needed cheering up more than anyone! True, some of the other children did seem to have more wrong with them than she had, but they all seemed remarkably happy. They seemed to know each others' names, and share private jokes, and even play

The unwelcome package

games from bed to bed. To be fair, they had tried to make friends with her, too, at first. But Tracey didn't want to be friends with anyone. She hadn't answered when they talked to her, and after a time they'd given up trying.

That night she was more miserable than ever. Nobody understood how horrid it was for her to be in hospital at this time. She tried to explain this privately to Nurse Davis. 'It's much, much worse for me than for any of the others, you see. I ought really to be having a lovely holiday now. A special one for Brownies. And I'm a *Sixer*! I'd have been helping our Brownie Guider to show the others —'

But Nurse Davis had stopped listening. She was staring at Tracey in surprise. 'You're a *Brownie*?'

'Yes,' said Tracey, 'I was telling you. And a Sixer, and I've got three badges and —'

'Well, well, well,' said Nurse Davis, almost as if to herself. 'A Brownie. I never would have guessed it!'

And there was something about the way she said the words that made Tracey feel very uncomfortable indeed.

7 · New ideas

'What d'you mean?' she asked, squirming under the bedclothes.

'You just don't seem like a Brownie to me,' said Nurse Davis.

'Of course I don't, in pyjamas,' said Tracey, 'but you should see me in my uniform with my tie and badge and Venture badge and —'

'Oh, I'm sure you'd *look* like a Brownie,' said Nurse Davis. 'That's not very difficult, is it?'

'It can be. You try ironing your tie and polishing your shoes before every meeting, and hanging up your tunic, or folding it properly to pack.'

'I have,' said Nurse Davis. 'I used to be a Brownie myself.'

'Oh. Oh, I see,' said Tracey in rather a small voice.

'Then I was a Guide,' said Nurse Davis.

New ideas

'Were you really?' said Tracey in a smaller voice still.

'And then I was a Brownie Guider.'

'I didn't know that,' said Tracey in a very small voice indeed.

'So one way and another I know quite a bit about Brownies.'

'Of course. Yes. You would,' agreed Tracey. Just think, Nurse Davis a Brownie Guider and she'd had no idea! Knowing this made her wish she could disappear under the sheets altogether. For deep down inside herself, Tracey knew that she'd been behaving in a very un-Brownie way indeed.

'Of course it's very difficult to remember you're a Brownie all the time,' said Nurse Davis as if she knew what Tracey had been thinking. 'Especially when the rest of the Pack isn't there to help you out.'

'Especially when it isn't there because it's having such an interesting time somewhere else.'

'But I'm sure they haven't forgotten you. Think what a lot they'll have to tell you when they come back.'

'They've done that already.' Tracey pointed to her package. 'All those letters in there are from the Pack Holiday.'

'Good gracious!' Nurse Davis picked it up. 'What a long time they must have taken to write.'

77

The Brownies in hospital

'And there are drawings too,' said Tracey. 'Would you like to see them?'

Nurse Davis looked at everything. She was amazed when Tracey admitted she hadn't bothered to read all the letters herself before.

'I thought it would make things worse, you see. Me being so out of it. But now I actually feel as if I'd been there, don't you? I wish I'd seen Ann fall into the river! I'd have made sure we won the sports, though. And trust Rosemary to burn the scrambled eggs!'

'You'll have to answer all these,' said Nurse Davis at last, packing the letters back into their envelope.

'But I couldn't possibly.'

'Why not? They couldn't each expect a separate answer but you could write one thank you letter, couldn't you? And perhaps your Brownie Guider could read it aloud at the next meeting.'

'I'm sure she would!' Tracey brightened at the idea. Then her face fell again. 'But the letters were full of funny things, and I've got nothing to say.'

'Nothing to say! Have all the Brownies in your Pack been to hospital then?'

'None of them that I know of.'

'Then think how interested they'd be to hear all about it.'

New ideas

Tracey considered. 'They might. Bits. But nothing much *happens* does it?'

Nurse Davis laughed. 'Things are happening all the time to somebody.'

'Not to me. I just have to lie here waiting to get well.'

'Tracey.'

Tracey looked up.

'You haven't forgotten the Brownie Guide Law, have you?'

'Of course not: "A Brownie Guide thinks of others before herself and does a good turn every day." Everybody knows *that*.'

'But does everyone put it into practice? Who have you been thinking of ever since you came here to be made better? I'll tell you. Of *Tracey*. The ward is full of children, and most have much more wrong with them than you have. Some have been here for weeks, even years, and are not ready to go home yet. Some can't sit up. Some can't write because of hurt hands. Some are too young to read. They're all longing to make friends with you.'

'But I don't even know their names.'

You've only to ask. The boy on your left is Wilfred. He has a back which wasn't formed properly. We're

The Brownies in hospital

hoping to make it better for him. On your other side is Susan. She had an accident.'

'What sort of an accident?'

'You can ask her yourself tomorrow,' Nurse Davis stood up. 'I must go. I'm supposed to be meeting a friend soon.'

Tracey longed to ask her to stay just five minutes more. Then she remembered that she should be thinking of others before herself. Nurse Davis worked long hours, and deserved her off-duty time.

'It's going to be a bit difficult to do good turns though,' was all she said.

'Don't you believe it. Once you get to know people, good turns will pop up all over the place. You'll see.'

Even before she opened her eyes next morning, Tracey found herself feeling quite different. At first she couldn't think why. Then she remembered her conversation with Nurse Davis. She heard again her words. 'A Brownie. I never would have guessed it!' And felt hot with shame. She'd let down her Pack badly. Suppose the others ever got to hear of her behaviour. Or worse, Miss Anderson?

There was only one thing to be done about it. She must be such a good Brownie from this minute onwards that everyone would forget what she'd been like before.

New ideas

At breakfast time she ate every scrap of what she was given. After all, a Brownie ought to set a good example to others.

Poor Wilfred had to be helped to eat because he was lying flat on his back. Tracey leaned towards her other neighbour. 'Hello, I'm Tracey.'

'I know,' said Susan. 'You got knocked by a car, didn't you?'

'Yes, but not too badly. What happened to you?'

The Brownies in hospital

'I fell out of a window.'

'A *window*?' Tracey was horrified.

'Not a very high one, but it was concrete underneath. I say, I'm glad you're in a talking mood today. I thought you were never going to be.'

'Yes. Well. I am,' said Tracey, not too anxious to discuss her moods. 'Is that snakes and ladders you've got there? If we could put a board between the beds on a chair, we could play.'

'Better than that,' said Nurse Davis. 'We've got a chariot for you today, Tracey. You can go and see people.'

The chariot was a wheelchair that she could propel along by herself. It was quite a struggle to get herself planted into it. Her big white plastered leg stuck out straight before her. It was more difficult to control than she'd expected, too, till she got the knack of steering. When she could go forwards and backwards and round in small circles, Sister in charge of the ward said she could go on a round of visits.

It was fun exploring the ward which she had so far only seen from her bed at one end where the older children were. The other held lines of cots where much smaller children lay. Most of them looked quite happy in spite of bandages and plasters, and grinned at

New ideas

Tracey when she appeared. She played for some time with various fluffy animals and floppy dolls (a hard toy is not comfortable for a baby to be in bed with).

Then she went to see the older children: Eddy, with a hip injury. Tom and Percy next to each other, both so nearly well they were always in trouble for being mischievous. Anna and Dot had become great friends. Anna had hurt her right hand and Dot her right wrist. They were practising writing with their left hand in large straggly letters.

Though Tracey asked everybody how they had come to be in hospital, people were more interested in what they had managed to do since they had been there. She realized that the ward was more a place for getting better than for feeling sorry for yourself.

By the time she had made friends with everybody, her own one broken leg seemed a very minor injury, so many people had more serious ones. Wilfred had been in the ward, on and off, for months, and it would be many more before he would go home. Valerie knew she wouldn't walk again for a long long time, but she never mentioned it.

When Sister told Tracey it was time to go back to bed to have dinner, she was amazed. Where had the morning gone? But she had to admit she was glad to

The Brownies in hospital

sink back against the cool pillows. It was odd to think that just sitting in a chair and talking to people could make you tired, but it was so. She ached all over, especially in her arms. She managed to eat her dinner, but only just, before she fell asleep.

Generally she spent rest time lying and feeling miserable. But today, when she woke up it was with a feeling of looking forward to something pleasant. What was it? Oh, yes, she and Eddy had planned a game of 'Heads and Bodies and Tails' and afterwards she was going to help Valerie with her jigsaw.

She glanced across the quiet ward, but they were both asleep. So were Wilfred and Susan. For a moment Tracey wondered what to do with her new lively-feeling self. Then she reached for the packet of Brownie letters, and read them through again, giggling softly. What a good time they were having! It had been kind of them to interrupt their holiday to write. She smiled at Sharon's lopsided words and dreadful spelling: 'I have been stinged by a hughg wosp!' There was a drawing by somebody else of Sharon, looking very small, and the 'hughg wosp' looking as large as a jumbo-jet.

Tracey stared for a long time at the photos. The Brownies were wearing shirts and shorts because they were on holiday. Some of the faces she did not recognize.

New ideas

'The Pack will have made a lot of new friends in the village,' she thought, but not enviously, because now she was making a lot of new friends as well.

'I say, Trace, what are you looking at?' Susan had woken up.

Tracey showed her the pictures and letters. Susan wanted to know more about Brownies. 'They sound good fun. Can anyone join?'

'If you've got a Pack near you.'

Soon they were talking. Tracey didn't notice two people enter the ward and pause for an inquiring word with Sister.

So it was with surprise she heard her say. 'You'll have to stop gossiping for a minute, Tracey. I believe you have some visitors you aren't expecting!'

8 · Surprises

'... So I'm afraid your visit may be rather a disappointment,' said Tracey's mother, pouring out second cups of tea all round.

Miss Anderson sipped hers. 'It's not like Tracey to be miserable for long.'

'It's not like Tracey to be miserable at all,' said Jane, her fellow-guest. 'She absolutely bounces.'

'Well, she hasn't been bouncing this week, I can tell you,' said Johnnie. 'Twice I went to see her, but not again. She didn't even bother to listen to a thing I told her.'

Jane wondered privately if the things Johnnie had told Tracey would have been of interest to her. About football, probably, and things the boys in his class had been up to. 'She's sure to want to hear all about the holiday,' she said hopefully.

Surprises

'I wouldn't be too certain even of that,' Tracey's dad said.

Jane stared at him.

Tracey's mum gave him a warning look.

'She didn't seem to care much about all those letters ... you ... sent ... a-hrrm!' His voice died away to an embarrassed mumble as he caught his wife's eye. 'Well, I mean she did, of course, but she didn't – in a manner of speaking.' He took a gulp of tea.

'She didn't,' Johnnie stated flatly. 'That's what you told me, anyway. Wouldn't even look at them.' He added to Jane, 'If you ask me, she's making a great fuss.'

'That's enough, Johnnie,' his mum said quickly. 'Another biscuit, Miss Anderson? I'm afraid it's true. Tracey isn't taking much interest in anything. Even those lovely letters and pictures you sent. In fact —' she hesitated, then evidently decided to go on. 'In fact she said thinking about you all made things *worse*.'

'Oh dear,' said Jane. 'I ought to have thought of that. I do see how it *could*.'

'Depends which way you're looking at things,' said Miss Anderson. 'It sounds as if Tracey isn't —' Then it was *her* turn to break off. She finished her tea and said. 'Thank you so much,' to Tracey's mum. 'I think Jane and I should be on our way now.'

The Brownies in hospital

'Give her our love,' said Tracey's mum.

'Tell her we'll be in tomorrow,' said her dad.

'Don't tell her I will be because I'm not going. Not till she bucks up a bit,' said Johnnie.

Jane decided she'd have to find a better way of putting that message before she delivered it.

She left the table rather nervously. She'd been so looking forward to visiting Tracey with Miss Anderson on behalf of the Pack. Now she wasn't at all sure that she wanted to go. As soon as she'd had that thought, she was sorry. 'We've got to think of *others* before ourselves,' she reminded herself. 'Tracey's one of the others this time.'

On the last afternoon the Pack had searched the fields and hedges for wild flowers to make a bunch for Tracey. Miss Anderson warned that they would not stay fresh for very long, but the Brownies were so *sure* that flowers from the real country would give Tracey what they called 'the feel of the holiday' more than anything, that their Brownie Guider had not stopped the bunch from being picked.

Already, in spite of spending the night up to their necks in a jug in Jane's house, a lot of the flowers were wilting. Jane looked anxiously at the hanging heads.

The Brownies in hospital

'Like what?' asked Jane, relieved that her Brownie Guider had thought of this.

'If you don't mind, I'm so very busy this week, because of having been away, that I'd rather like the chance of a quick word with Tracey tonight in any case. As you *could* come another evening, perhaps, if she's not feeling quite herself, you might leave early?'

Jane nodded. She understood exactly what was meant. Sometimes a 'quick word' with a Brownie Guider could put a lot of things right. And if that was the kind of word Miss Anderson meant, it might be better if Jane were not there.

They turned two corners and saw the hospital, with its special red brick wing for children. Jane swallowed and wished they could walk more slowly. Miss Anderson went on at a normal pace.

Inside the hospital were hospital smells which reminded Jane of the day of the ambulance, and she shivered. She didn't know, as Tracey knew by this time, that such smells are generally connected with getting well.

'Poor Tracey,' said Jane as they climbed the stone stairs to the ward. 'It must have been awful for her. I'm sure I'd have been miserable too.'

Surprises

'Do you think it's worth taking them?' she asked Miss Anderson as they left Tracey's house together.

'Most of them will survive at least one evening,' she answered. 'And they still smell lovely.'

That was true. The bunch had the sweet strong country smell that Jane would never forget.

Miss Anderson had found a cottage that sold pots of home-made honey and bought one for Tracey. Hearing her mother talk about Tracey's not eating made her worry about that present too. Suppose honey were the last thing she wanted? Or the last-but-one. (The last being wild flowers.) She sighed.

'Cheer up!' said Miss Anderson. 'We shan't be able to brace Tracey up if we're downhearted ourselves!'

They came to the High Street. To the very place where the accident had happened. They used the crossing, looking very carefully in both directions before they did so.

'I'll never forget that day. Never,' said Jane.

'So you'll never have the kind of unnecessary accident Tracey had,' said Miss Anderson in her matter-of-fact way. 'Now then, suppose she still isn't in the mood for visitors? We'd better have a plan of campaign, don't you think?'

Surprises

'Perhaps she won't be, now,' said Miss Anderson. Jane thought she didn't sound too hopeful.

They came to Ward 'C'. Tracey's ward.

Jane stopped walking. 'You go in first,' she said, clutching the flowers with hot hands.

Miss Anderson went into the ward. At once a tall person in uniform came towards them.

'Good afternoon, Sister,' said Miss Anderson at once as if she went into unfamiliar hospital wards every day. 'Could we see Tracey Robinson please?'

'Of course,' said Sister leading the way to Tracey's bed. Jane heard her say. 'You'll have to stop gossiping for a minute . . .'

And then there was Tracey sitting up, laughing away like anything with the girl in the next bed. The coverlet was strewn with papers she remembered very well. There was her own writing, and Rosemary's drawings. Tracey was holding up Sharon's letter. The bed shook with giggles.

There was time only to exchange very quick astonished looks with Miss Anderson before Tracey saw them.

Her face became an enormous beam.

'*Jane!* Miss Anderson. Oh, how lovely! We were just

The Brownies in hospital

talking about you. Oh, this is Susan. Sue, this is our Brownie Guider, and Jane...'

Jane stared. Where was the depressed miserable creature they had heard so much about? What about the lack of interest in the Brownie letters? They were everywhere.

'Mum and Dad are all right, aren't they?' Tracey asked suddenly anxious. 'And Johnnie?'

'Fine,' said Miss Anderson. 'They kindly let us come on our first opportunity to give you all the news, that's all.'

'I can't *wait*!' said Tracey. 'Do sit down. This is Wilfred... Honey! My favourite! Oh, *thank* you. We'll all have some for tea tomorrow.'

Jane stepped forward with the flowers. 'From everybody,' she said.

Tracey's nose dived straight into the middle of the bunch. 'Mmm! Heavenly smells, all mixed. D'you know I can hardly believe you're back yet!'

'You've been here more than a week,' Miss Anderson reminded her.

'Have I really?' A nurse passed, smiling. Tracey called out to her. 'Nurse Davis, do look at my lovely flowers. *And* honey. They're from —' Jane, watching Tracey, saw her turn a little pink, but she went on '— from my Brownie Guider and the Pack.'

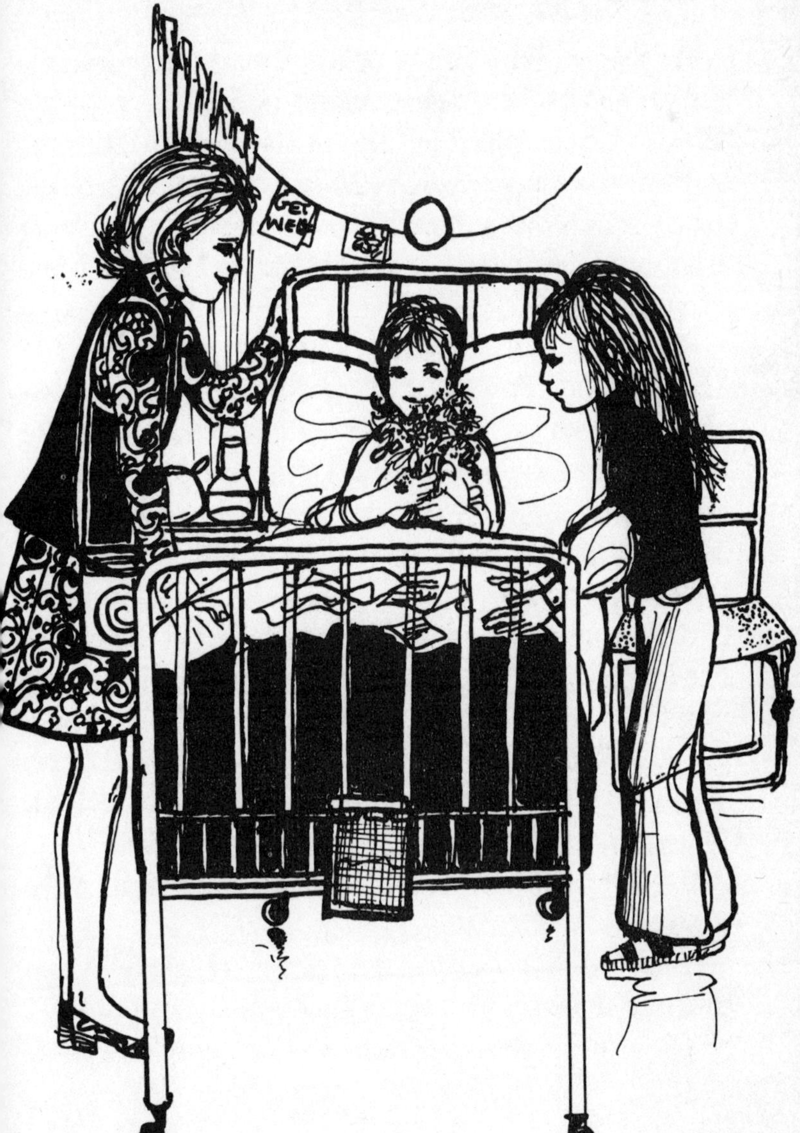
GET

The Brownies in hospital

As soon as she said the words, Tracey's face became pinker and pinker. Jane couldn't understand it at all. Was Tracey ashamed of them or something?

Even more mysteriously, Miss Anderson and Nurse Davis were staring at each other in the way people do who think they have met before, but are not sure when or where.

Then they both suddenly said 'Downland Training Camp!' and burst out laughing. It seemed that they *did* know each other. Tracey seemed more agitated than ever. As Nurse Davis and Miss Anderson moved away for a quiet word with each other, Jane whispered, 'What ever's the matter? Your face looks like a tomato.'

'It feels like it,' said Tracey putting her hands on her cheeks. 'Jane, the most awful thing —' She looked round swiftly to make sure no one else could hear. Susan quickly hid behind a book to show she wasn't interested. Wilfred was talking to his father who had just arrived. 'Nurse Davis has been a Brownie Guider herself!'

'I don't see what's so awful about that. It must make it nicer —'

'But I didn't *know* – it might have made things different if I had. You don't know, you can't think —'

The usually bouncy Tracey was certainly in a state.

Surprises

Jane thought she'd better hear what it was all about. 'Start at the beginning,' she ordered.

Tracey took a big breath. 'The beginning. Well, you know all about *that*. More than anyone.' She paused.

'Get on with it,' said Jane hastily.

'It was afterwards. Everything was so horrid. You know, missing the Pack Holiday. And it was so sunny outside and hot in bed. And everything hurt, and – well, Jane, you can't think how nasty I was.'

'What sort of nasty?' Jane inquired cautiously.

'Every sort. I wouldn't talk to anyone. No one at all. Even poor old Mum and Dad.'

Jane nodded. 'Or Johnnie.'

'How d'you know?'

'Sorry. Go on.'

Tracey looked puzzled for a moment, but then continued, 'They brought presents and I wouldn't say thank you properly. I didn't even read your letters for ages. And — Oh, never mind. Just think of the awfullest way anyone *could* behave, and that was me!'

'It surely wasn't as bad as all that, because —'

'It was,' said Tracey solemnly.

'But look at you now!'

'I'm better now, much.'

'What —?'

The Brownies in hospital

'Nurse Davis. When I told her I was a Brownie, she could hardly believe it.'

'Because —?'

Tracey nodded. 'Because.'

'Oh, how dreadful!'

'And she said – well never mind about what she said. But about the Law and things – you know.'

Jane nodded. She could imagine all too well. Poor Tracey!

'And the very last thing I wanted was for Nurse Davis to meet Miss Anderson, and look at them, jabbering away like anything!'

'But not about you,' said Jane watching them. 'More old times and other people they both know.'

This seemed to be true. Tracey cheered up a little. Soon Nurse Davis had to go on with her duties. Miss Anderson came back to Tracey's bed. 'Wasn't that extraordinary, meeting an old friend like that? I hadn't seen her for years. She says you're getting on splendidly, by the way, Tracey.'

'Did she, really?' (Oh, kind Nurse Davis!)

After that the visit flashed by. Of course Miss Anderson was introduced to all Tracey's friends who didn't happen to have visitors of their own just then. Jane and Miss Anderson took it in turns to tell stories

Surprises

about the holiday and soon that end of the ward was rocking with laughter and Miss Anderson said they'd better go before Sister quite rightly chased them out for making so much noise.

'Please, come again!' Tracey begged. 'If it's not too much trouble. And Jane, give my love to them all at home and say – say I'm looking forward to seeing them.' She lowered her voice. 'Aren't they nice, all the people in bed? Some of them will have to stay here for ages. Isn't it a shame that they can't be Brownies too?'

'But they can!' said Miss Anderson.

9 · Home-coming

Tracey and Jane stared at her.

'How?' asked Tracey at last. 'I mean, they couldn't go to meetings.'

'They can't even get up, some of them,' Jane pointed out.

'They couldn't possibly get a uniform on, the people with plasters,' Tracey added. 'And what interest badges could they take?'

'Oh, plenty,' said Miss Anderson and Jane, and then laughed because they'd spoken at exactly the same time.

'It isn't everyone who likes the running and jumping kind that you do,' Jane reminded Tracey. 'Think of Knitter or Needleworker or Brownie Friendship —'

'— Or Writer or Book Lover or Artist or Collector,' Miss Anderson said. 'There's even a swimmer's test for people who aren't well enough to take the ordinary one. And don't forget that though interest badges are fun

Home-coming

to take, they aren't the most important part of being a Brownie.'

No, thought Tracey to herself. That was one thing she would *not* forget now.

'But if they can't have meetings —' Jane was saying slowly. 'I mean there are a lot of things they can't do aren't there?'

'All the more reason for them to have a chance to do the others,' said Miss Anderson. 'Brownies in hospital, or who live at home but are handicapped, aren't forgotten. They can be helped in all sorts of ways to feel they belong.'

Tracey actually bounced in bed, forgetting for a moment about her leg. 'Then do let's make all the girls here who are the right age into Brownies, now, this minute!'

'Not so fast —'

'But they'd love it so! Think how they enjoyed hearing about our holiday —'

'Tracey,' said Miss Anderson. 'Be reasonable. Quite a number of the children here will be going home soon. By all means encourage them to join near-by Packs – one of them might be ours. But I wouldn't say too much to the others if I were you. For one thing, there are parents to be consulted, aren't there? And for another,

The Brownies in hospital

we don't know what arrangements there are round here for helping handicapped Brownies.'

'Can't we find out?' Jane was almost as eager as Tracey.

'Of course we can, and I will. Now I really must be off. See you again soon, Tracey.'

She was gone.

Jane stayed a little longer. There was so much to talk about, and it was such a relief to find Tracey was her old self again.

After Jane had gone, Tracey lay back, her mind buzzing with ideas. Perhaps when Susan was out of hospital, she could join their own Pack. Perhaps even be in Tracey's Six. That would be fun. She began to count on her fingers the others in the ward who might later become Brownies. She went to sleep that night with a sigh of contentment.

Directly after breakfast next morning she wrote an answering letter to the Pack. Jane had promised to come and fetch it so that Miss Anderson could read it out at the very next meeting.

'Dear Everybody,' began Tracey. 'Thank you for all your letters and photos and drawings and the flowers, they are on my locker now. They smell lovely.'

She paused, to think for a minute, before going on:

Home-coming

'Jane came, and Miss Anderson, and told us all about the holiday. Everybody here fell about laughing. I think some of them may be Brownies when they come home.'

'What are you so busy at, Trace?' Susan wanted to know.

Tracey explained.

Susan had an idea. 'I say, you let us hear all *their* letters, so why don't we all write to them?'

Everybody thought this was a good plan. So when Tracey's chariot had arrived she was kept busy handing round pieces of paper and hunting for pencils and Biros. Soon everybody was scribbling.

'Just like we wanted to hear about their holiday,' said Tracey (forgetting that at one time she hadn't), 'they'll want to know about what it's like inside the hospital'.

So the letters described all the funny things that had happened in the ward since Tracey had been there, and the drawings were of each other.

There were pictures of Sister and of Nurse Davis and of Wilfred eating breakfast flat on his back. Some of the pictures were very odd, and come to that so was the writing – especially the left-handed efforts. But it all caused a great deal of laughter. When Sister and Nurse Davis came to see what it was about they were shown their portraits.

The Brownies in hospital

'Good gracious!' said Sister. 'Do I really look as fierce as that?'

'Sometimes,' said Valerie, who had known Sister a long time. 'But you never really mean it.'

Nurse Davis thought that if she was as fat as she appeared in Susan's portrait of her, she'd better take more exercise to lose weight; but she helped Tracey put all the letters together so that Jane could take them away.

Next day was an exciting one for Tracey. In the morning Dr Martin said. 'It's nearly time we got rid of you! What about seeing how you get on with a pair of long crutches?'

'Crutches? Yes *please*, I'd love to!'

'I thought you would. Very well, Mrs Warner from the physiotherapy department will show you how to use them later this mornings.'

'But I know how to use crutches!' said Tracey laughing.

'You haven't had to before, have you?'

'No, but I've seen other people – and – oh, *everybody* knows how to use crutches!'

The extraordinary thing was that when the moment came she found that *everybody didn't* know how to use crutches. Mrs Warner, who was stout and grey and patient, was not in the least surprised by this. 'It always

Home-coming

takes practice the first time. After you've got the knack, you'll wonder why you had to learn it.'

At first Tracey found it difficult even to balance.

The Brownies in hospital

'How peculiar,' she said, 'you'd have thought that with an extra leg it would be easy at least to stand up!' But even as she said it she sat down suddenly on the bed for the third time she hadn't meant to.

Going along was tricky too. 'Move the crutches forward first,' said Mrs Warner, an arm round Tracey. 'Now a little hop forward on your good leg and let the other swing through —'

But the clumsy plaster leg didn't want to swing through at the right moment and Tracey was glad to be able to sway against Mrs Warner. There came one moment after she had taken several successful steps when she suddenly couldn't remember what to move next. Was it the crutches' turn, or the good leg or —? She stood feeling foolish for long enough for Susan to draw her, crutches straddled, legs wobbling and her mouth open in bewilderment.

'Like a spider gone balmy,' Tracey said indignantly when she saw it later.

'Just what you looked like,' said Susan.

At the end of the first attempt with crutches Tracey was tired and slightly cross with herself. But after her second she suddenly found she could swing along quite easily, if she muttered: 'Crutches – step – swing! Crutches – step – swing!' to herself. All the same, her

Home-coming

shoulders ached quite soon and she felt as if she'd climbed the highest mountain in the world, as she told Mrs Warner.

'Tomorrow we *will* climb!' was the answer. 'You shall try going up and down stairs.'

'Goodness,' said Tracey. 'What happens after that?'

'After that,' said Mrs Warner, 'we'll change you to a shorter lighter kind of crutch that fit under your elbows instead of your shoulders, and then you'll probably go home.'

'Home!' exclaimed Tracey, as if she had never thought of such a thing.

'Don't you want to go?'

Tracey thought of being at home with Mum and Dad, and Johnnie to argue with. Of her own little bedroom Of everything . . .

'Oh *yes*!' she said. 'Of *course* I do!'

All the same there was a part of her that would be quite sorry to leave the hospital. It was a strange, mixed feeling.

Another day went by. Tracey learnt how to manage steps, and walked up and down the entire length of the corridor. Then she got used to the new elbow crutches, which were less tiring.

The day after, Mum came to see her with a suitcase of

The Brownies in hospital

clean clothes, and Jane came with her to collect the Brownie letters. She was surprised and delighted to discover how thick the package was.

The day after *that* —!

'What, now?' said Tracey.

'After tea,' said Sister smiling, 'they're coming to fetch you.'

Tracey thought of the long roads between hospital and home. She remembered how she ached after walking the length of the corridor twice.

'I'm not sure I can get that far,' she said doubtfully.

'Your father said he's ordered a taxi,' said Sister.

A taxi! How very grand!

Half of Tracey couldn't wait to go home. The other half was sad, especially when it was time to say good-byes. 'But I'll come back,' she promised everyone. 'And so will Jane. And —' she longed to say something about Miss Anderson and about Brownies in hospital, but thought she had better not.

'— and don't you dare forget about me!' she finished in a threatening tone.

'We won't!' the other children said.

'As if we could,' said Sister. 'It'll seem so peaceful without you.'

Home-coming

Privately Nurse Davis added, 'And it's been nice to have a real Brownie in the ward.'

'But —'

'No, truly, you've cheered everyone up wonderfully in the last week. You've lent a hand in all directions. *And* done good turns.'

'Have I?' asked Tracey, honestly surprised. 'I wasn't exactly thinking about it —'

'I know. That's the best part.'

'D'you know,' Tracey confided, 'now it's time to go, I almost don't want to.'

'Always the same,' said Nurse Davis cheerfully. 'It's the people who take longest to settle in who —'

'— find it hard to settle *out*?' Tracey finished for her. 'It's not nice – all these good-byes.'

'Well, don't say "good-bye" to me.'

'Why not?'

Nurse Davis looked mysterious. 'You'll see.'

'But —'

'Don't talk so much. Isn't that your father coming in now?'

It was.

'Dad!' cried Tracey. Suddenly home seemed very real again, and hospital only a place she had had to stay a little while.

The Brownies in hospital

She stood up, and grasped her new crutches firmly; crutches – step – swing! Crutches – step – swing!

Sister came with her.

'Good-bye!' Came a chorus from the beds. 'Come back soon!'

'I will! I will.' She was suddenly choky.

'Baked beans waiting at home,' said Dad.

And they were off . . .

10 · *Looking forward*

The room buzzed and twittered with talk as seventeen lively Brownies collected for the Pack meeting.

'Tracey's coming today.'

'I know. She told me. I've seen her.'

'So have I. She let me have a go on the crutches, *and* I wrote my name on her plaster!.

'What are we doing today – does anyone know?'

'Tracey, does, or partly anyway.'

'What, then?'

'She wouldn't say.'

'It's a secret?'

The word 'secret' whispered round like a snake hissing. Suddenly everybody was in one group wanting to know it.

'What kind of secret?'

'Nobody knows.'

'Miss Anderson must.'

The Brownies in hospital

'Oh yes, *her*. And Tracey.'

'And Jane?'

'I don't know. She might. Look, she's talking to Miss Anderson now.'

'They're looking at lists on paper.'

'More letters from Tracey?'

'Not if she's coming, stupid!'

'Her new friends in hospital then. I'll bet it's something to do with them.'

'I heard Miss Anderson say something about "a Pack Venture".'

'Then it must be – look, here's Tracey!'

And there she was indeed, using her crutches as if she'd known how to all her life and grinning widely.

Everyone clustered round her. The talking and questions and laughing became even more shrill. When Miss Anderson, in the corner, said, 'I think that's everything settled then,' Jane knew what she said only by watching her mouth move.

Miss Anderson started the meeting by welcoming Tracey back. Nothing was said at this point about the care needed when crossing roads. Tracey had learned her lesson the hard way, and the Pack had discussed this seriously at a previous meeting before she had returned.

When the Pack gave her the Pack Welcome, Tracey

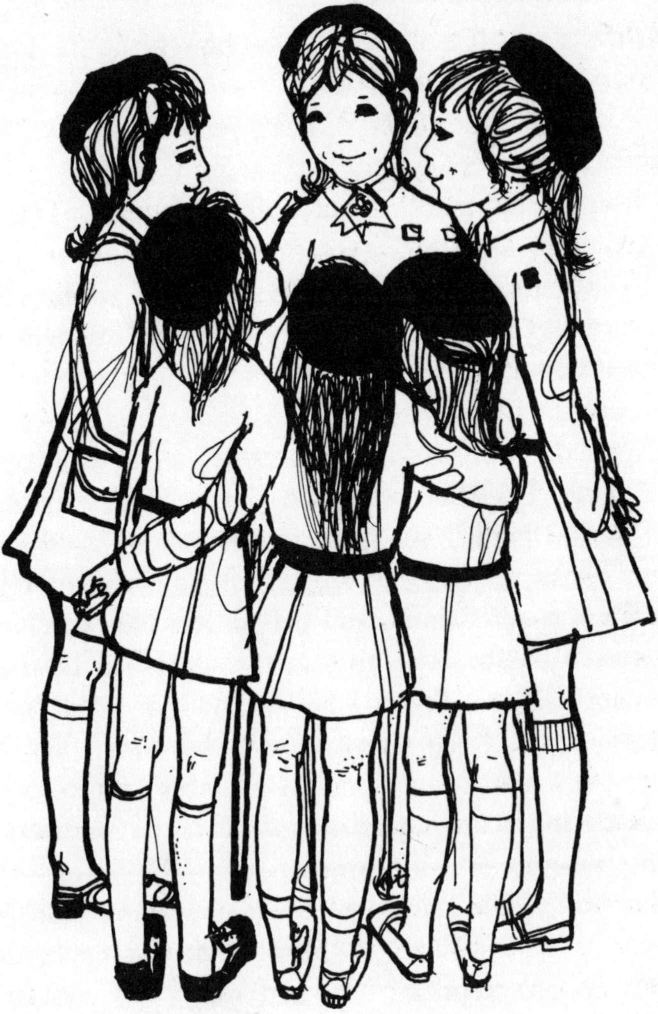

The Brownies in hospital

felt awkward. If only they knew how little, for some days, she had deserved it! It was a little like being treated as a heroine when you knew you weren't one. The real heroines were people like Valerie who had to stay in hospital for months, but didn't complain. Tracey would have liked to have said something about this, but she knew Miss Anderson was going to, so she only muttered 'Thank you,' rather pinkly, and thought to herself how lucky she was to have been made better so quickly.

Then their Brownie Guider came to the main part of her talk. It had been hard on Tracey to have to miss the Pack Holiday, she said, but something good had come out of her being in hospital. Miss Anderson told the Pack about Valerie, and people like her, and how interested all the little girls in the ward had been in Brownies. 'It was Tracey who realized how much *being* Brownies would help them, so, with her to nag me —' there was laughter; everyone knew Tracey's ways – 'I've been making lots of inquiries to see if we can make some of her new friends into Brownies.'

Lots of people wanted to know how they could be Brownies in Hospital, so Miss Anderson explained carefully. She went on: 'I've had a long talk with our Extension Adviser for the county, and it seems that in

Looking forward

"Tracey's" hospital there would be a good chance of forming a Pack.'

Now everyone was interested. The room was quiet as she continued, 'In hospital where a number of Brownie-aged patients have to stay for a long time, this is often a very successful idea. Pack meetings can be held actually in the ward, which means that people who have to stay in bed can join in too. Now then, I expect you've got lots of questions.'

Of course she expected right. Questions came thick and fast.

'Who'd be their Brownie Guider?'

'I would. I'd like to be.'

'Does that mean you'd have to leave us?'

'Not at all. I can run two Packs.'

Sighs of relief all round.

'What about badges?' someone asked. 'How would they get to the testers?'

'They wouldn't. The testers would go to them.'

'It's going to be a bit tricky for one or two of the patients,' Jane said slowly. 'Some of Tracey's friends stay in hospital for quite a long time, and then go home and then come back again. They'd get awfully left out while they weren't there.'

'Not at all!' said Miss Anderson cheerfully. 'You

113

The Brownies in hospital

know how handy letters are for keeping in touch! We'll let them know how we're getting on in hospital, and they can write back. Then when they return they can pick up where they left off.'

Tracey thought suddenly of her friends who were boys, or too old to be Brownies. 'Can the same be arranged for Cub Scouts, and Guides and Scouts, and if so —?'

Miss Anderson laughed. 'Steady, Tracey! One thing at a time. Let's get the Brownies started first, *then* perhaps we can encourage the others! As it is, there will be quite a lot of organizing to do. Luckily Miss Davis, who's a nurse in the ward at present, has promised to help me get started.'

(So that's why she didn't say good-bye!) 'I'll help too,' said Tracey, promptly. She turned to the others. 'We'll *all* help, won't we?'

'Ah,' said Miss Anderson. 'I was coming to that. I think it would help the new Pack if we took an interest in them. Suppose we "adopted" them as a Pack Venture?'

This idea was accepted enthusiastically, and there was a chance for everyone to discuss how the plan might best be carried out.

Tracey, as usual, was the centre of the group, full of

Looking forward

ideas, and how other people could help put them into practice.

Watching her, Jane found it hard to believe she had really been the sulky and uncooperative patient she had confessed to being. But she would never have owned up to such behaviour if it hadn't been true.

Miss Anderson, also watching the talkers from a little distance, said, 'Tracey has quite recovered her spirits, hasn't she?'

'Yes, thank goodness,' said Jane. 'It must have been awful for her – and everybody when she was – while she —' she faltered.

'We can forget all about that time now, I'm sure,' said Miss Anderson comfortably. 'But one thing we *must* think about. I've spoken to the parents of Susan, and several other short-stay patients, and it seems likely we shall have several more Brownies in our own Pack soon. We'll have a new Six, and I'm hoping that you'll be its Sixer.'

'Me?' Jane gaped in surprise. '*Me* – why me?'

'Why not?' said Miss Anderson.

Jane struggled to explain. 'I'm not a – a – Sixer sort of person.'

'That's a matter of opinion, perhaps?'

'You know what I mean. I don't mind being Second,

The Brownies in hospital

but I don't think – I can't – it's someone else like Tracey you need.'

'It's you, I need. You'll make a very good Sixer. You've proved that.'

'I have? How?'

'Who kept her head in an emergency and remembered how to send for the ambulance, and took Tracey's place on the holiday, and stuck by her afterwards? *That's* the sort of person I want.'

'Goodness,' Jane was turning the idea over. 'Tracey and I were going to join the Guides at the same time, so I thought I'd never —' All the same, to have a Six of her own! For the first time she felt a little bit proud.

'So you'll do it?' Miss Anderson was watching her.

'Well, I suppose – well, yes. Of course I'll try. Thank you for asking me.'

Suddenly she felt like popping. Exactly like a blown-up paper bag. She wouldn't just try. She'd *do* it. She'd be a *good* Sixer.

Just wait till she told Tracey!

There was no time to do this till they were walking home together. When Tracey heard the news, she was so surprised that she waved a crutch in the air and made a dignified old gentleman mutter 'Gently, gently' into his whiskers.

Looking forward

'You – a Sixer!'

'You don't mind, do you?' asked Jane anxiously. It would spoil everything if Tracey were cross about it.

'Mind? Why should *I* mind?'

'Well – I shan't be able to be your Second any more, remember.'

'Never mind that, Rosemary will be, I expect. A new Six? I wonder what we'll call it? Won't it be fun to

The Brownies in hospital

have so many new Brownies? And we'll have so much to do, with this new hospital venture. I've got masses of ideas —'

'So have I,' said Jane.

'— And you can help me do the things —'

'Not any longer. I'll help my own Six do my ideas.'

'What?' exclaimed Tracey. Then she laughed. 'I suppose you will!' They went to the edge of the road by the crossing.

They crossed very, very carefully.

On the far side of town, the hospital stood tall and gleaming rosily in a sunny sky.

Other Brownie titles:

THE BROWNIES THROW A PARTY *by Pamela Sykes*
THE SECRET BROWNIES *by Dorothy Richardson*
THE BROWNIE VENTURERS *by Dorothy Richardson*
THE BROWNIE ELEPHANT HUNTERS *by Dorothy Richardson*
THE BROWNIE CAMPAIGNERS *by Dorothy Richardson*